PACEMAKER®

Skills for Independent Living

GLOBE FEARON

Pearson Learning Group

Pacemaker® Skills for Independent Living, Second Edition

Executive Editor: Eleanor Ripp
Lead Editor: Brian Hawkes
Lead Designer: April Okano
Cover Designer: Tricia Battipede
Production Editor: Debi Schlott
Electronic Specialist: Leslie Greenberg
Manufacturing Manager: Mark Cirillo

About the Cover: People need many skills to successfully live on their own. The images on the cover represent a variety of these skills. "To Do" lists help people organize themselves. People's keys open their apartments, houses, and cars. Smart and healthful shopping helps people buy what they need. Bus and train schedules help people get to places on time. Finally, people need to earn money and stay on a budget. What are some other skills for independent living that people need? How could these skills be represented?

ISBN: 0-130-23823-6

Printed in the United States of America
8 9 10   09 08

Globe
Fearon

Pearson Learning Group

1-800-321-3106
www.pearsonlearning.com

Contents

A Note to the Student

Getting ready to live on your own may sound complicated. You will need to know how to get or find things for living independently. You will need to know how to prepare for the things that you will be doing on your own. This book was made to help you develop those skills.

This book will help to make your journey to living independently a success. Your journey will be comfortable and interesting. You will build new skills based on what you already know. You will make connections between the skills that are taught in this book and the real world. As you work through the exercises and practice sections in this book, you will build the skills you need to live on your own.

Each chapter presents concepts through clear explanations of real-world experiences. The chapters give you chances to try out your skills in the **Practice** sections. Then you move on and use those skills in the **You Decide** features. Notes in the margin have also been included to connect the chapter to different parts of your life.

There are many other study aids in the book. At the beginning of each chapter, you will find **Learning Objectives**. They will help you focus on the important points covered in the chapter. You will also find **Words to Know**. This is a look ahead at new vocabulary you will learn. At the end of each chapter, you will find a **Vocabulary Review** and a **Chapter Quiz**. These will help you review what you have just learned. A **Unit Review** also comes after each unit.

Everyone who put this book together worked hard to make it useful, interesting, and enjoyable. We wish you well on your journey to living independently. Our success comes from your success.

Unit **1** ▷ # Focus on You

Chapter 1
Getting to Know Yourself

Chapter 2
Setting Goals

The way a person looks is only a small part of who that person really is. What are the qualities and beliefs that also make you who you are?

Learning Objectives

- Describe your appearance, interests, and skills.
- Describe beliefs that are important to you.
- Explain how people use their beliefs to make decisions.
- List the steps in wise decision making.
- Give examples of being responsible at school, at home, and at work.

Chapter 1 / Getting to Know Yourself

Words to Know

honesty	the ability to be truthful and fair
responsibility	the ability to be dependable, to make wise decisions, and to accept the results of your actions and decisions
courage	the strength to stand up for what you know is right
concern	an interest in other people
respect	the willingness to consider other people's needs, feelings, and opinions
health	mental and physical wellness
citizenship	active, helpful membership in a community
independent	able to take care of yourself

In the situations below, Maria and Tony each have to make a difficult decision. What they decide will tell a lot about who they are and what is important to them.

"Maria," Susan says, "do you want to come to my party on Saturday?" Maria is excited that Susan asked her. Then Susan adds, "Don't say anything to Courtney, okay? I can't invite everyone." Courtney is Maria's best friend. Now Maria is not sure she should go.

Tony is trying to ignore Monica, who is sitting beside him in science class. "Please, Tony," Monica whispers. "Let me see your answers on the test. If I don't get at least a C, the coach won't let me play Friday." Monica is captain of the girls' basketball team.

1-1 ▸ Deciding Who You Really Are

If you asked Maria or Tony who they are, they might give you their names and ages. Maria could add that she has a friend named Courtney. Tony might say that he likes science. All of these are important descriptions. Yet, they do not describe who these people *really* are.

How you look and what you like to do are only a small part of who you are as a person. A bigger part of who you are includes your beliefs about what is important. These beliefs guide your decisions and your actions each day. These beliefs guide your life.

Look back at the decisions Maria and Tony must make. Before they can make these decisions, they must think about what is important to them. Maria must decide whether a party or her friend is more important. She must decide whether it is important to become part of the popular crowd.

Tony also has to decide what is more important to him. He must decide whether he should help the school win the basketball game by letting Monica cheat or keep his promise to himself not to help others cheat on tests.

Practice

On a separate sheet of paper, describe yourself. Write down what you look like, where you live, and where you go to school. Add anything else you think is important about you. Save this paper so you can read it later.

1-2 ▸ Understanding Important Qualities

After Maria and Tony think about what is important to them, they will be ready to make their decisions. Many people think the qualities on page 5 are important. Having these qualities helps people gain the respect, trust, and admiration of others.

1. **Honesty** is the ability to be truthful and fair.

2. **Responsibility** is the ability to be dependable, to make wise decisions, and to accept the results of your actions and decisions.

3. **Courage** is the strength to stand up for what you know is right.

4. **Concern** is an interest in other people.

5. **Respect** is the willingness to consider other people's needs, feelings, and opinions.

6. **Health** is mental and physical wellness.

7. **Citizenship** is active, helpful membership in a community.

Did You Know ?

Some schools have a "code of honor." Every student promises to tell the truth and be honest at all times. Honesty helps the students gain the trust and respect of others.

Practice

Choose one of the seven qualities above. On a separate sheet of paper, write how you could tell that someone has this quality.

1-3 ▸ Deciding What Is Important to You

Our families and friends help us decide what is important in our lives. Keith remembers how he learned that honesty is important. When Keith was only six, he took a candy bar from a store without paying for it. When his mom found out, she made him take the candy bar back. She also made Keith tell the clerk he was sorry. Keith says he was embarrassed. Yet, this helped him learn that honesty is important. He also learned to be responsible for his mistakes.

You need to figure out which qualities you admire. Knowing this will help to shape your beliefs and

Think About It

People learn many of their values and beliefs from their families. What values and beliefs have you learned from your family?

Your family helps shape your values and beliefs.

decisions. It will also help you become the kind of person you want to be. You might not want to be friends with someone who has not thought about what is important in his or her life. It would be difficult to listen to or trust this person's advice.

Practice

Choose a quality that is important in your life. On a separate sheet of paper, explain how your actions show that this quality is important to you.

1-4 ▸ Taking Steps to Make Wise Decisions

Thinking about what is important in your life can help you make decisions. However, making decisions can still be difficult. The steps below can help you make those difficult decisions. You do not need to follow these steps for easy decisions, such as what to eat for lunch. However, these steps can help you make difficult decisions.

STEP 1 Identify the decision you need to make.

STEP 2 List as many choices for your decision as possible. If you have many choices, you will have a better chance of making a wise decision.

STEP 3 Cross out choices that are harmful or go against your beliefs.

STEP 4 Read each remaining choice. Think about what might happen if you select it.

STEP 5 Select the choice that will probably have the best results for you and others.

STEP 6 Carry out your choice.

STEP 7 Think about the results of your decision. That way, you will know whether to select that choice the next time.

Using the Steps

Think back to Maria's situation. Susan had invited Maria to a party. However, Susan did not invite Maria's best friend, Courtney. Now Maria must make a difficult decision. Here is how the decision-making steps could help her make the decision.

STEP 1 **Identify the decision Maria must make.**
Maria must decide whether to go to Susan's party.

STEP 2 **List Maria's choices.**
a. Maria could tell Susan she cannot come.
b. Maria could go to the party and not tell Courtney about it.
c. Maria could go to the party and tell Courtney about it.

STEP 3 **Cross out choices against Maria's beliefs.**
If Maria went to the party without telling Courtney, she would not feel honest. Maria crosses out choice b. If Maria went to the party and did tell Courtney, she would hurt Courtney's feelings. Maria crosses out c.

STEP 4   **Think about what might happen for each remaining choice.**
Only one choice is left. Maria can tell Susan she cannot come. If Maria does this,
- she might miss some fun and a chance to become part of the "in crowd."
- Susan may not invite her to another party. However, if she does not go to the party, Courtney will not feel left out.

STEP 5   **Select the best choice.**
Maria would like to go to Susan's party, but Courtney's feelings are more important to her. Maria decides to skip the party.

STEP 6   **Carry out the best choice.**
Maria tells Susan that she cannot come to the party.

STEP 7   **Think about the possible results of the decision.**
On the night of the party, Courtney and Maria go skating and have a great time. Maria is sure she made the best choice. Courtney's friendship is much more important to her than a party.

Practice

Suppose you were Maria. On a separate sheet of paper, write what you would have done. Which steps helped you most in deciding?

1-5   Getting Ready for Responsibility

Most young people want to make their own decisions. But some people are not ready to make their own decisions as soon as others. They are ready when they show they are responsible. Responsible people make wise decisions that help themselves and others. Responsible people also do what they promise they will do.

Everyone makes mistakes. However, responsible people admit their mistakes. Then they do what they can to make up for their mistakes. For example, Lorna borrowed Jeannie's shirt. Then she accidentally dripped ketchup on it. Lorna did not try to hide the spots. Instead, she washed the shirt before she returned it. If the spots had not come out, she would have bought Jeannie a new shirt.

Responsible people accept the results of their decisions. A teenager named Lisa knew that taking orders over the phone might be a boring job. However, she took the job because it paid well. After only two weeks, she hated going to work. She could have complained about being bored. She could have taken sick days when she felt fine.

▶ **Everyday Tip**
Always act responsibly. Your friends, parents, teachers, and employers count on you to do the right thing.

Instead, Lisa reminded herself that she had chosen that job. Now she is looking for a more interesting job. But she always reports for work on time and does her best. Like other responsible people, Lisa does not blame others for her decisions or actions. Instead, she tries to learn from her decisions. That way, she can make a wiser decision the next time.

Responsible people do not expect others to solve the problems that they have caused. Mike, for example, often missed the bus because he slept late. Yet, he did not expect his parents to drive him to school. Mike rode his bike to school, even in the rain. Each time he missed the bus, he made sure to get up earlier the next day.

No Excuses, Please

A responsible person does not make an excuse to hide his or her mistakes. An excuse is an explanation for poor behavior. People who make excuses often blame someone else for their own mistakes. They are trying to make themselves look good. However, they are not being responsible.

When Pete was caught cutting class, he could have blamed his friends. After all, they had begged him to leave school with them. But Pete knew it was his own decision to go along with his friends. So Pete did not make excuses for cutting class. When his teacher made him stay after school, Pete did not complain. He knew his own decision had gotten him into this situation. Pete made a bad decision to cut class, but he acted responsibly by not making excuses.

Responsible people are also honest. Kay is honest, sometimes. For example, she would never steal something from a store. But Kay takes pens at work. She thinks no one will miss the pens she takes. She is making excuses for stealing. Kay is not being honest or responsible. Her employer may soon stop trusting her.

Rodney believes it is all right to take extra-long breaks at his job. Rodney makes excuses by telling himself that he works hard. He needs time to relax. But if his boss catches him wasting time, she will only see that Rodney is not doing his job.

No matter what excuses people give, they are judged by what they do. Their actions, not their words, show what they think is important.

Taking on Responsibility

Sometimes responsibilities are given to you. You might be chosen as the leader of a team. You might be asked to prepare dinner on Tuesdays and Thursdays.

Other times, you might volunteer for responsibilities. Maybe a friend is struggling with an oral report. You might offer to listen to it and help improve it. You might volunteer to drive your younger brother or sister to soccer practice on the weekends.

Being responsible means doing your share—and a little more. When you do that "little more," you will feel good about yourself. Others will notice. Being responsible has many rewards. At home, you might be able to make more of your own decisions. At school, you might improve your grades. At work, you might get a raise.

Practice

On a separate sheet of paper, write the headings below. Then fill in the information. You may be surprised at how responsible you are.

Responsibilities	Assigned to Me	Accepted on My Own
At Home		
At School		
At Work		

1-6 ▸ Getting Acquainted With Yourself

Look back at the way you described yourself in the Practice on page 4. Now you know there is more to you than what you first listed.

Now you might also list the qualities that are important to you and that guide your life. These could include honesty and caring about others. You might also mention that you know the steps in making wise decisions. You could also list ways that show you are responsible.

These qualities and skills are your personal strengths. In this book, you will explore more of your skills. You will also add to the skills. The skills you gain and strengthen will help you become more **independent**. Independent people are able to take care of themselves. This course will help prepare you to meet your own needs and handle challenges that come your way.

Practice

In what ways are you independent? On a separate sheet of paper, describe at least three things you do that show you are able to take care of yourself.

Summary

Your beliefs about what is important are part of who you are. These beliefs guide the decisions you will make in your life.
Most people think these qualities are important in life: honesty, responsibility, courage, concern for others, respect for others, good health, and good citizenship.
Seven steps can help you make wise decisions. These steps help you think of possible choices and the results of each choice. Then you can select the choice that will probably have the best results for you and others.
Responsible people admit their mistakes and accept the results of their decisions.
Responsible people do not make excuses for their poor decisions.
Knowing what is important to you, being able to make wise decisions, and being responsible are skills that will help you become independent.

Vocabulary Review

honesty
concern
responsibility
health
courage
independent
respect
citizenship

Complete each sentence with a term from the list. Use a separate sheet of paper.

1. If you stand up for what you know is right, you show _____ .

2. Your mental and physical wellness is your _____ .

3. People who are _____ can take care of themselves.

4. An active, helpful member of a community shows good _____ .

5. When you are truthful and fair, you show _____ .

6. Having an interest in other people is called _____ .

7. People who show _____ accept the results of their actions.

8. _____ is the willingness to consider other people's needs, feelings, and opinions.

Chapter Quiz

Write your answers in complete sentences.

1. What are some ways that people might describe themselves?

2. What are seven qualities that many people think are important in life?

3. Honesty is important to Rosa. She bought a sandwich that cost $3.50. However, the clerk asked her for only $3. What should Rosa do? Why?

4. Mike and Lon came to a party together. A friend offered Mike a ride home. However, there was no room in the car for Lon. What are Mike's choices?

5. Mike takes the ride and leaves Lon behind. Then Mike tells himself that he never told Lon they would leave together. What is Mike doing?

6. What are two actions that show responsibility at school, at home, or at work?

7. **CRITICAL THINKING** What are three reasons people act in responsible ways?

Writing Activity

In most states, 16-year-olds can drive cars. Do you think all 16-year-olds are responsible enough to drive cars? Why, or why not? Explain your answer in a paragraph on a separate sheet of paper.

Group Activity

You agree to baby-sit on Friday night. Then a friend invites you to a big party on the same night. Should you baby-sit or go to the party? With a partner, follow the steps on page 7 to decide what to do. Then share your decision with the class.

Sometimes people work together to reach a goal. What is one goal that you can achieve with the help of someone else?

Learning Objectives

- Describe how our priorities affect our goals.
- Explain why having goals is important.
- Identify goals that are specific and realistic.
- Describe the difference between a short-term and a long-term goal.
- Write an action plan to meet a goal.
- Create a daily schedule to manage your time.
- Explain ways to avoid wasting time when studying.

Chapter 2 / Setting Goals

Words to Know

goal	something you want to do
priority	a level of importance
obstacle	something that stands in the way of reaching a goal
specific	clearly described
realistic	within your reach
long-term goal	a goal you expect to reach in several months or years
short-term goal	a goal you expect to reach in a few hours, days, or weeks
action plan	a list of steps to help you reach a goal

In the story below, two friends have a goal. Find out which one reaches the goal, and why.

One Saturday morning, Eric and Dana wait at a city bus stop. They both want to go to the high school, but the bus is very late. Eric is picking up a CD he left in his locker. Dana is meeting with the volleyball coach.

Dana's neighbor drives by and tells them that she has just seen the bus up the street. There was smoke coming from its engine.

"There goes our ride," Eric says. "I guess I'll wait until Monday to get that CD. See you!"

Dana frowns. It will take half an hour to walk, so she walks quickly. When Dana gets to the school, she is just a little late for her meeting.

A **goal** is something you want to do. As Eric and Dana waited for the bus, they both had the same goal. They wanted to get to the high school. However, when the bus broke down, Eric gave up on his goal. He did not care enough about getting his CD to walk to school.

Dana really wanted to get to the high school. Being on the team was very important to her. That is why she was so determined to meet with the coach. She was willing to walk several miles to school.

Think About It

When you know what is important to you, you can set goals. What are some of your goals?

When a goal is important in our lives, we give it a high **priority**. A priority is a level of importance. Setting priorities means putting things in order of their importance. A goal may have a high priority for one person, but not for someone else.

Eric put a low priority on getting to the school. He gave up when he met an **obstacle**. An obstacle is something that stands in the way of reaching a goal. The obstacle in Eric's way was the bus's breaking down.

Dana put a high priority on getting to the school. The higher the priority we give a goal, the more important it is to us. When the bus broke down, Dana did not give up. She overcame the obstacle by walking to the school.

Obstacles do not have to keep you from reaching your goals. When a goal is important to you, you can find ways to overcome most obstacles. For example, you might baby-sit to get enough money to buy a gift for a friend.

Practice

On a separate sheet of paper, list two goals that have a high priority for you. Write why each goal has a high priority in your life.

Goals give our lives purpose. People without goals tend to drift along without a clear direction. They might drop out of high school. If they do not have goals, graduating might not seem important to them.

However, five years from now, these dropouts might meet friends from high school. These friends did set goals. They graduated from high school, gained more training, and now have good jobs. The dropouts might call these friends "lucky." Yet, setting goals is not a matter of luck. Setting goals is a skill that can help you become independent.

Setting Specific Goals

Jill has set a goal of getting in shape. However, she does not know where to start. She also does not know how she will know when she has reached her goal. Jill's goal needs to be more **specific**. A specific goal is clearly described. It can be measured.

Suppose Jill gets out of breath when she climbs stairs. Her specific goal might be to walk up three flights of stairs without running out of breath. To work toward this goal, Jill might join an exercise class. She will know she has reached her goal when she gets up to the third floor without huffing and puffing.

Did You Know ?

The more specific your goal is, the better your chance of reaching it.

Practice

Decide which of the goals below are specific. List the specific goals on a separate sheet of paper.

1. I want to get better grades.

2. I want to get a B on my next math test.

3. I want to be popular.

4. I want to make one new friend each week.

Forming Realistic Goals

If you set a goal that is specific and important to you, you may or may not reach it. You need to choose a goal that is also **realistic**. To be realistic, a goal has to be within your reach. It has to be a goal you can meet with your own skills.

For example, Kevin dreams about buying a new car in a year. He has already picked out the model he wants. This goal is important to Kevin. It is also specific. However, Kevin must decide if it is realistic.

Kevin earns $50 a week at his part-time job. He has $375 in the bank. Kevin writes down the price of the car he wants and adds gas, insurance, and other costs. He can see he does not have enough money for a new car. He understands his goal is not realistic. Instead, Kevin begins looking for a used car that he can afford.

Short-Term and Long-Term Goals
Getting an interesting, full-time job after high school is an example of a **long-term goal**. A long-term goal is one you expect to reach in several months or years. Buying a car is another long-term goal for many people.

A **short-term goal** is one you expect to reach in a few hours, days, or weeks. Finishing an art project by Friday is a short-term goal.

▶ **Everyday Tip**
Make sure your goals are important to *you*, not to someone else.

Many long-term goals can be broken into smaller short-term goals. For example, raising a grade from a C to a B is a long-term goal. You could meet this goal by setting smaller goals. One smaller short-term goal might be studying an hour longer for each test.

Practice

On a separate sheet of paper, list three short-term goals and three long-term goals for yourself. Explain why the goals you listed are specific, realistic, and important.

Making an Action Plan

After you have set a goal, you need to make an **action plan.** An action plan is a list of steps that will help you reach your goal. The following are steps for making an action plan.

STEP 1 **Write down your goal.**
Write your goal in your journal or diary. Or write your goal on a sheet of paper and tape it to the mirror in your bedroom.

STEP 2 **List steps to reach the goal.**
Break a long-term goal into several smaller goals. Break smaller goals into steps.

STEP 3 **Set up a timeline.**
Decide how much time each step should take. Then write each step on a chart or calendar. Keep track of the steps on your chart.

STEP 4 **Identify any obstacles.**
List things that might get in the way of your goal. Write ways you might overcome them.

STEP 5 **Identify sources of help.**
Decide who or what could help you reach your goal. You and a friend might help each other work toward the same goal.

STEP 6 **Check your progress.**
As you work toward your goal, review your plan. Check whether you are on schedule. If your plan is not realistic, make changes so you can still reach your goal.

Practice

Look back at the short-term goals you listed in the Practice on page 18. Choose one of these short-term goals. On a separate sheet of paper, use the steps above to write an action plan to meet that goal.

Managing Your Time

Now you have set goals and made an action plan. But what if you don't have time to follow your plan? Knowing how to plan your time is a valuable skill. It helps you to reach your goals. You do not have to schedule every minute of the day. However, planning your time can help you reach important goals.

To make the best use of your time, follow these steps.

1. On a separate sheet of paper, make a "To Do" list of the things you *have* to do and *want* to do tomorrow. Things you *have* to do might include school assignments, meetings, tutoring, part-time work, and sports practices. Then add things that you *want* to do or that your family, friends, and others *want* you to do. All these tasks are possible goals for tomorrow.

2. Mark each item on your list *A, B,* or *C,* according to the descriptions below.

   A. These are very important tasks that have the highest priority and must be finished.

   B. These are important tasks that should be started or worked on.

   C. These are not-so-important tasks that can be put off for another time.

To Do List
Finish book report for tomorrow — A
Take dog for a walk after school — A
Watch favorite program on TV — C
Go to soccer practice — A
Check sale at CD store — C
Start studying for test on Friday — B

A "To Do" list tells you what you need to do.

3. On a second sheet of paper, divide the day into 30-minute periods. Start with the time you get up. End with the time you go to sleep.

Time Schedule
3:00   Go to soccer practice
3:30   (still at soccer practice)
4:00   Get home and walk dog
4:30   Start book report

A time schedule tells you when you need to do things.

4. On your schedule, write in all the *A* activities from your list. Then fit in as many *B* activities as possible. If you have room, add some *C* tasks. Remember to allow enough time for each activity, including travel and clean-up. Set aside time for fun, and do not try to schedule every minute.

5. Follow your plan tomorrow. Notice whether you get more done. If you fall behind schedule, make a more realistic schedule for the following day. Allow more time for the activities that took more time than expected. Planning your time may help you get so much more done that you decide to make a schedule for every day.

Wasting Time

Wasting time is often an obstacle to reaching a goal. Finishing homework is an important goal for all students. You might sometimes find that you work for a long time and do not finish an assignment. There are many reasons why that might happen. They are all time wasters.

Each time waster can be managed. Interruptions can keep you from getting your work done. To avoid them, don't answer the phone. Work in a quiet corner away from friends, family members, and the television.

If necessary, explain to others that you are busy and will have time to talk later. Daydreaming is another way of interrupting yourself. Take five minutes to daydream. Then get back to work.

Avoid redoing projects and reports. Ask questions when your teachers give assignments. Make sure you understand what to do. Then you can do the assignments right the first time.

Forgetting necessary materials can also waste time. Make sure you have pens, paper, and other supplies at home. Keep a list in a notebook of books and materials you need to take home. Then check your list before going home.

Using Technology

If you work on a computer during the day, save your work on a disk. Then you will have it to work on later, and you will not waste time.

Practice

Talk with a partner about ways that students waste time when studying. Write down which time waster is the biggest problem for you. How can you avoid wasting time in this way?

2-6 ▸ Choosing a Path

Setting a goal is like choosing a path to follow through a forest. Without a goal, you might wander into the trees and get lost. You could end up going in circles. Setting goals gives your life a clear direction. You know where you are going. You also know when you have gotten there. As you overcome obstacles, you build self-confidence. Then you can set bigger goals—and reach them.

Practice

On a separate sheet of paper write at least two goals that you plan to accomplish in the next month.

YOU DECIDE
How to Use Time Well

Read the situation below. Then follow the steps to help Jan decide the best use of her time.

It is 5:00 P.M. Jan needs to study at least two hours for tomorrow's history test. However, the tryouts for the school play are also tonight. They will take place from 7:00 P.M. until 10:00 P.M. Jan thinks she wants to be an actress. Being in the play could help her decide on a career. At the same time, she wants to do well on the history test. She must decide what to do.

On a separate sheet of paper, follow the steps below to help Jan decide the best use of her time tonight.

STEP 1   Identify the decision Jan must make.

STEP 2   List Jan's choices.

STEP 3   Cross out any choices that might be harmful or against Jan's beliefs.

STEP 4   Think about the possible results of the remaining choices.

STEP 5   Select the best choice.

STEP 6   Explain how Jan would carry out that choice.

STEP 7   Describe the possible results of Jan's choice.

Make a Difference
What would you tell Jan about going to the tryouts?

Summary

The more important a goal is, the harder people are willing to work to reach it. People give important goals a high priority in their lives.

Goals can give your life direction. To be helpful, goals must be specific, realistic, and important to you.

A short-term goal might be met within hours, days, or weeks. A long-term goal might take months or years to reach.

An action plan breaks a goal into steps. It also sets a timeline for each step.

To plan your time, start by listing all the tasks to be done. Then give each task a priority. Do the most important tasks first.

Time wasters include interruptions, daydreaming, having to redo projects, and forgetting needed materials.

Vocabulary Review

obstacle

realistic

goal

action plan

specific

long-term goal

short-term goal

priority

Write the term from the list that matches each definition below. Use a separate sheet of paper.

1. something you want to do

2. a list of steps to help you reach a goal

3. a level of importance

4. within your reach

5. a goal you expect to reach in a few hours, days, or weeks

6. something that stands in the way of reaching a goal

7. clearly described

8. a goal you expect to reach in several months or years

Chapter Quiz

Write your answers in complete sentences.

1. Jamal has set a high priority on getting a summer job. Akim has made it a low priority. Which person is more likely to get a job this summer? Why?

2. Kate set a goal of getting along better with her younger sister. What is a more specific goal for Kate?

3. What can happen if you set a goal that is not realistic?

4. What is one example of a short-term goal and one example of a long-term goal?

5. How can making an action plan increase your chances of meeting a goal?

6. Name one time waster that can occur while you study. How can you avoid this time waster?

7. **CRITICAL THINKING** Some people get more done than other people. Why might that be so?

Writing Activity

Your friend is ready to graduate from high school. He explains that he might not have enough money to go to college or a technical school. He says, "I'm thinking about just looking for a job. What do you think I should do?" On a separate sheet of paper, offer your friend advice about setting goals.

Group Activity

Manuel wants to help his older neighbors with their household tasks. That is a large, long-term goal. On a separate sheet of paper, write two or three smaller goals Manuel could set for himself to reach this large goal. Work with a partner and report to your class.

Unit 1 **Review**

Read each sentence below. Then choose the letter that best completes each one.

1. A skill that could help a young person become more independent is
   A. being responsible.
   B. making wise decisions.
   C. knowing what is important.
   D. all of the above

2. All of the following qualities are important in life except
   A. honesty.
   B. selfishness.
   C. respect.
   D. courage.

3. When people are responsible, they
   A. admit their mistakes.
   B. accept the results of their decisions.
   C. do not make excuses for their poor decisions.
   D. all of the above

4. All of the following are steps in an action plan, except
   A. listing steps to reach the goal.
   B. setting up a timeline.
   C. identifying any obstacles.
   D. giving up your goal.

5. When you manage your time well,
   A. you are more likely to reach your important goals.
   B. you schedule every minute of your day.
   C. you make the basketball team.
   D. you make lots of friends.

6. All of the following are time wasters except
   A. daydreaming.
   B. interruptions.
   C. remembering needed materials.
   D. having to redo projects.

Critical Thinking

How can setting goals help you live on your own and be independent? **WRITING** Write a short essay about the decisions you have to make when you plan your time. Tell how to make sure you reach your goals. Be specific with your examples.

Unit **2** **You and Others**

Chapter 3
Dealing With Peer Pressure

Chapter 4
Communicating With Others

Chapter 5
Getting Along With Others

Chapter 6
Handling Change and Stress

Friends respect each other, learn from each other, and have fun together. How do true friends help each other during difficult times?

Learning Objectives

- List questions to ask yourself when choosing friends.

- Give examples of positive and negative peer pressure.

- Explain ways to tell the difference between positive and negative peer pressure.

- Give examples of ways to resist negative peer pressure.

Words to Know

popular	admired or wanted as a friend
pressure	to strongly encourage
peer pressure	influence from people your age to do or not do something
positive	helpful or healthful
negative	harmful, unsafe, or against the law
resist	to refuse; to say "No"

In the situation below, Jake's friend is forcing him to make a difficult decision.

"Jake, I just need this one favor," Marco begs. "All you have to do is tell my mom I went to the movies with you last night."

"But you didn't!" says Jake. "I was home doing my report. My mom knows that. What if your mom says something to my mom about us going to the movies? Then I'll be in trouble for lying!"

"Well, I can't tell my mom I was hanging out on 18th Street last night, can I?" asks Marco. "Not after she told me to stay away from there. If you won't help me, I won't be your best friend any more."

You may spend a lot of time with your friends. Friends can share fun and talk over problems. However, friends can also force you to make hard decisions. Jake has to make a difficult decision. He must decide whether he should lie for Marco or tell the truth. If Jake does not lie for Marco, Jake may lose him as a friend. If these two cannot talk through the problem, Jake may need to find a new friend. Jake needs to choose friends who will not force him to do something he does not want to do.

Looking for New Friends

When people look for friends, they might consider the most **popular.** Popular people are those who are most admired or wanted as friends. They might include class leaders or star athletes.

Some young people might be popular because others like them or admire something about them. Being friends with popular people can be fun. However, popular people have to divide their time among many friends. That could rule out a close friendship with you.

To find a new friend, talk to people you see every day but do not really know. Start by saying "Hi" to someone in your classes or neighborhood. Get to know the members of groups you belong to. They might share some of your interests.

Deciding Whether Someone Is a Friend

You need to know when you have found a new friend. A friend respects and likes you for who you are. A friend would also help you when you need help. Most importantly, a true friend does not try to force you to do things you do not want to do.

A friend is someone you feel comfortable with. This person will not try to make you act or dress in a certain way. A friend will not try to make all of your decisions or be upset if you have different opinions.

It is also important to respect a friend. You should choose friends who have qualities that you feel are important. For example, a friend who believes honesty is important will not ask you to lie. Choose friends who respect your values and beliefs.

Relationships sometimes last longer if you have activities that you both enjoy and can share. However, having friends who enjoy very different activities can also be enjoyable. You might be able to teach each other new skills or share new ideas and experiences.

▶ **Everyday Tip**
A new friendship can begin with a simple smile. Try it.

Choose your friends wisely. Do not make the mistake of choosing someone just because you think he or she will make you look cool. If you have nothing in common and cannot rely on that person, the friendship will not last.

Practice

On a separate sheet of paper, list three reasons why you would want to be friends with someone. Then list two ways you could be a good friend to that person.

3-2 ▶ Identifying Peer Pressure

Your friends may often ask you to do things. One friend may **pressure**, or strongly encourage, you to go to the basketball game on Friday. Another friend may want you to join a club that meets in the evening.

These demands are examples of **peer pressure**. Someone your age is asking you to do or not do something. Peer pressure is **positive** when the activities suggested are helpful or healthful. For example, suggesting that you never cut class is positive peer pressure.

Some of your friends might pressure you in **negative** ways. Negative peer pressure is encouragement to do something harmful, unsafe, or against the law. For example, someone might pressure you to start smoking. Giving in to negative peer pressure often leads to problems.

Practice

On a separate sheet of paper, list three examples of peer pressure. Trade lists with a partner. Talk about the examples in your lists. Decide which you think are positive peer pressure and which are negative.

3-3 Determining Positive and Negative Peer Pressure

It is important to recognize whether a friend's pressure is positive or negative. When a friend suggests an activity, you need to decide whether it goes against your beliefs. Ask yourself whether the activity makes

Did You Know ?

Peer pressure is a part of life that everyone faces, no matter how old they are.

These girls feel positive peer pressure as part of a team.

you feel uncomfortable. If it does, it is probably negative peer pressure.

Another way to decide whether something is negative peer pressure is to consider if the activity a friend is suggesting is unsafe. If the activity could be dangerous for you or someone else, it is a form of negative peer pressure.

Ask yourself why you want to go along with an activity that someone is suggesting. If you just want to take part in the activity to be accepted, you are giving in to negative peer pressure.

Make your own decisions about what you want to do and about the things that make you comfortable. A true friend will respect your feelings.

If your answer to any of these questions is "Yes," the peer pressure is negative. You need to **resist,** or refuse, the pressure by telling your friend "No." You might be risking a friendship. However, giving in to negative peer pressure can cost you other people's trust.

Carla paid a high price for giving in to negative peer pressure. She let Greg copy a book report she had written. The teacher recognized Carla's report. Carla and Greg were both called to the principal's office and given failing grades. Greg did not care; he was used to being in trouble.

After Carla was caught cheating, things changed for her. She soon realized that her teachers no longer trusted her. She could not ask them to help her get a scholarship for college. She might not be accepted to a college without their help.

Remember
Knowing what is important to you and being able to make wise decisions are valuable skills.

Practice

Think of a situation that could involve positive peer pressure or negative peer pressure. On a separate sheet of paper, first explain how this situation could involve positive peer pressure. Then explain how the same situation could involve negative peer pressure.

It is important to learn how to work well with others. This skill is important in the workplace. Employees need to be able to work well with each other. You also need to practice making your own decisions. Employees who can make wise decisions often get raises and better jobs.

Last summer Terrence, Eduardo, and Gerald worked on a road construction crew. One hot afternoon, Gerald said to Terrence and Eduardo, "It's too hot. Let's get some ice water and take a break under that big tree over in the field." Without a word, Terrence followed Gerald. Eduardo knew it wasn't time for their break for another hour, so he kept working. The crew supervisor found Gerald and Terrence half an hour later relaxing against the tree. What was Terrence's excuse? "Gerald made me do it!"

Gerald was fired because he did not make a wise decision. Terrence was fired because he did not make his own decision. He went along with Gerald because he didn't know how to say "No."

▶ **Everyday Tip**
If you do not know whether to say "Yes" or "No" to a friend's request, talk it over with someone you respect.

There are many ways to say "No" to negative peer pressure. For instance, do not agree to something before you know what is being suggested. Suppose a classmate asks for help with a test. Before you say "Okay," make sure your classmate wants to study together, not copy your answers.

Say "No" calmly and confidently. Do not embarrass or anger the person asking. Simply look the other person in the eye. Use a firm voice to show that you have made up your mind. Then the person should stop pressuring you.

If you want to spend more time with this person, suggest a positive activity instead. For example, you might say, "Cutting school to go to a movie could get us in trouble. Let's go to a movie tonight instead."

Practice

On a separate sheet of paper, describe a time when you or someone you know did not give in to negative peer pressure. What did someone want you to do? What did you say or do? What, if anything, would you do differently the next time?

3-5 Providing Positive Pressure

Sometimes even good friends suggest negative activities. Many young people want to try things they have been told not to do. Gayla, for example, knows that stealing is wrong. Yet, it seems exciting.

Gayla is in a store with Erica. "Erica," Gayla whispers, "Let's both take a pair of earrings and hide them in our pockets. I bet no one will catch us."

Erica's mouth drops open. "Are you crazy?"

Gayla shrugs and smiles. "I was just kidding."

The truth is, Gayla really did not want to steal the earrings. But she might have done it if Erica had agreed to steal. She really hoped Erica would say "No." Gayla needed and wanted Erica's positive peer pressure to keep her from making a bad decision.

When Negative Pressure Continues

Erica knew Gayla would still be her friend if she refused to steal the earrings. But sometimes people might not respect your feelings. If you say "No" to them, they might not want you in their group. If you say "Yes," you will probably be allowed in the group. A real friend will not pressure you to do things you do not feel comfortable doing. A real friend respects you and your decisions.

Think About It

Why might you want to practice responses like these? "I don't want to do that." "I've decided not to do that." "I have to go now."

Watching for Hidden Pressure

Sometimes the one applying negative pressure is you. For example, Jamie did not smoke cigarettes. Only one boy, Kevin, among his new friends was smoking. Kevin seemed to be the group's leader. Kevin must think smoking is cool, Jamie told himself. If I smoke, he'll want me in his group. Jamie asked Kevin for a cigarette.

Kevin handed him one and said, "I'll give you one, but you shouldn't smoke. I've been trying to stop. I want to run on the track team again." Kevin looked at the other guys. "I'd better never catch any of you smoking!"

Embarrassed, Jamie handed back the cigarette. "I don't really smoke," he admitted. The next time, he will make sure that he is telling himself what he really wants.

Friends and Peer Pressure

It is natural for people to want to have friends and be part of a group. Still, the need to be accepted can lead to problems. Some young people begin to ignore what they think is important. They let others guide their decisions and actions.

Some people are so afraid of losing friends that they forget they have choices. They do not have to do what a friend or a group does. They can make their own decisions. If you are sure of yourself and what is important to you, it will be harder for others to get you to do something you know is wrong.

If making your own decisions costs you friends, you can replace them with better friends. Join a club or team to meet new people. New friends can help you feel accepted again.

Using Technology

Some Internet service providers have sites for young people to share solutions for dealing with peer pressure.

Practice

On a separate sheet of paper, describe a situation in which you could use positive peer pressure to help a friend make a good decision.

Read the situation below. Then follow the steps to help Gabe decide what to do.

Anthony and Gabe have picked the movie they want to go to tonight. "Let's see if Victor wants to come with us," Gabe suggests.

"Nah!" says Anthony. "We'd probably have to pay for him to get in. Victor never has any money. Let him stay home." Gabe knows that Victor's father lost his job. Victor works part-time, but he gives all the money he earns to his family.

On a separate sheet of paper, follow the steps below to help Gabe decide what to do.

STEP 1   Identify the decision Gabe must make.

STEP 2   List Gabe's choices.

STEP 3   Cross out any choices that are harmful or might be against Gabe's beliefs.

STEP 4   Think about the possible results of the remaining choices.

STEP 5   Select the best choice.

STEP 6   Explain how Gabe would carry out that choice.

STEP 7   Describe the possible results of Gabe's choice.

Make a Difference
What would you tell Gabe about inviting Victor to the movies?

Summary

A true friend respects and likes you for yourself. This friend also respects the things you feel are important. Friends share some of the same interests.
Positive peer pressure encourages you to do something helpful and healthful.
Negative peer pressure is encouragement to do something that goes against your beliefs. This activity may be harmful or illegal.
Friends can apply positive or negative pressure.
If you give in to negative pressure, you let others make your decisions and control your actions.
If someone suggests a negative activity, say "No," calmly and confidently. Suggest a positive activity instead.
Sometimes when friends suggest a negative activity, they actually hope you will say "No."
People sometimes apply negative pressure on themselves. They need to be careful not to talk themselves into joining a negative activity.

Vocabulary Review

Write *true* or *false* after each sentence. If the sentence is false, change the underlined word or words to make it true. Use a separate sheet of paper.

1. A <u>positive</u> action is harmful, unsafe, or against the law.

2. To <u>pressure</u> is to encourage strongly.

3. <u>Peer pressure</u> is influence from friends to do or not do something.

4. Someone who is <u>popular</u> is admired or wanted as a friend.

5. A <u>negative</u> action is helpful or healthful.

6. To <u>resist</u> something is to refuse or to say "No" to it.

Chapter Quiz

Write your answers in complete sentences.

1. What are three questions to ask yourself when choosing friends?

2. Would a true friend insist that you wear a certain brand of jeans? Why or why not?

3. Sandy knows that Keisha lies to her friends sometimes. Would Sandy and Keisha make good friends? Why or why not?

4. What are some ways to find new friends?

5. Filipe wants Antony to go to the mall. How could this be positive peer pressure? How could it be negative peer pressure?

6. What might happen if a teenager gave in to negative peer pressure at a part-time job?

7. **CRITICAL THINKING** What should you do if a good friend suggests a harmful activity? Why?

Writing Activity

Do you think adults feel peer pressure? On a separate sheet of paper, write a paragraph about how peer pressure could affect adults.

Group Activity

Meet with two classmates. List three examples of positive peer pressure you have experienced. Then list three examples of negative peer pressure on you or others. As a group, describe which you think is stronger—positive peer pressure or negative peer pressure.

Communicating includes listening as well as speaking. How do good listeners show they understand the speaker's feelings and care about what the speaker is saying?

Learning Objectives

- List actions that can discourage someone from speaking.

- Explain how to be a good listener.

- Describe how people communicate with body language.

- Explain how people in different cultures communicate differently.

- Explain how being thoughtful helps people be better communicators.

Chapter 4 — Communicating With Others

Words to Know

communicate	to share thoughts, feelings, and ideas with others
advice	suggestions about what should be done
express	to show your thoughts, feelings, or ideas
summarize	to explain briefly the main ideas of what you heard, saw, or read
body language	showing feelings using your body and your face

In the situation below, Angelo needs someone to listen to him. Decide whether you think Larry is a good listener.

Angelo and Larry are in the locker room after football tryouts. Angelo shakes his head. "I really messed up today," he tells Larry. "I slipped twice, and I nearly missed that long pass."

"Hey, did you see what happened to me?" Larry asks. "I dropped the ball! But the coach knows that was an accident."

"I don't think I'm going to make the team," Angelo says sadly. "My dad will be really disappointed if I don't play football. He played for three years on his high school team. My brother . . ."

"Your brother played football?" Larry asks.

Angelo shakes his head. "No, but he . . . "

"Hey, maybe you should try out for track."

When people **communicate**, one person explains a thought, a feeling, or an idea. Another person listens and understands the thought, feeling, or idea. Keep in mind that communicating is more than just one person talking. It also requires a listener.

Larry was not listening to Angelo. Larry had no idea how upset Angelo was about the tryouts. Larry could have listened to Angelo and encouraged him to talk about his feelings. Instead, Larry talked about himself.

Angelo needs a friend who not only talks but also listens. Listening is an important part of being a friend. A friend is willing and able to listen when you have uncomfortable or happy feelings to share.

Being a good listener takes some practice. You can be a better family member, friend, and employee by strengthening your listening skills. This chapter will help you get started.

Recognizing Poor Listening Skills

You can tell when someone is not listening to you. Maybe the person is looking around the room or watching television. Not listening can also be shown in other ways. Some people just wait for the speaker to finish talking. Then they jump in and tell their own story. They often talk about when the same thing happened to them, only it was worse.

Think back to when Angelo said he almost missed the pass. If Larry had been listening, he would have noticed how upset Angelo was. Instead, Larry pointed out that he did something worse—he dropped the ball!

Larry told Angelo he should have gone out for track instead of football. Angelo didn't ask for Larry's **advice**, or suggestions about what should be done. He was hoping that Larry would just listen to him.

Think About It

Think of the people you like to talk to. They are probably good listeners. What makes them good listeners?

Telling people what they *should* have done, or should *not* have done, is not good listening. Unwanted advice can discourage speakers from talking. Good listeners wait until someone asks for their advice.

Some people have a habit of finishing other people's sentences. When Angelo said, "My brother," Larry thought he knew what Angelo would say next. Many speakers stop talking when others keep interrupting them.

Practice

Talk with a partner about the ways that people show they are not listening. Write down the ways. Then share them with the class. Discuss how people feel when others do not listen to them. Remember not to mention the names of any specific people.

4-2 Learning Skills for Good Listening

Now you know some ways people show poor listening skills. Poor listening discourages people from talking. Good listeners encourage people to **express** themselves. To express means to show your thoughts, feelings, or ideas. Here are some good listening skills.

1. Good listeners look at the speaker. They also show they are listening by turning their bodies to face the speaker. Sometimes good listeners lean toward the person who is talking. Good listeners show that they care about what the speaker is saying.

2. Part of listening is letting the speaker talk. Good listeners do not interrupt the speaker. If the speaker stops to take a breath, they do not jump in and start talking. Instead, they wait until the speaker has finished what he or she wants to say. Even if a good listener has something important to say, he or she waits for the right time to speak.

▶ **Everyday Tip**
Looking at the speaker is important. Think about how you would feel if people turned away while you spoke.

3. Asking questions is another way to practice listening skills. Good listeners do not just sit silently. When the speaker is finished talking, they ask questions. Asking questions shows they are interested in what the speaker has to say. For example, the listener might ask:

"What happened then?"

"What do you think she will say?"

"What will you do about that?"

Remember
When you respect people, you consider their needs, feelings, and opinions.

4. Noticing the speaker's feelings shows that you are listening to what he or she has to say. To be a good listener, try to understand the feelings behind a speaker's words. For example, a friend might say, "My sister is getting married." You can ask questions to find out how the friend feels. You might ask, "Are you looking forward to the wedding?" You could also ask, "Do you like the man your sister is marrying?" or "Will you miss her when she moves away?"

5. Listeners can also show that they understand the speaker's feelings. Some ways to do that are by saying, "That sounds exciting," or "That would bother me, too."

To be able to **summarize** what the speaker said is another good listening skill. To summarize means to explain briefly the main ideas of what you heard, saw, or read. Summarizing what people said is a way to see whether you understood them. One example of summarizing is, "I see. You wanted to explain what happened, but he wouldn't let you." Another example of summarizing is, "So you think the experiment will work if you make that change?"

6. Good listeners also give the speaker a chance to clear up any misunderstandings. They might ask the speaker, "Is that right?" You do not always have to summarize what a person says. In some conversations, it would be annoying. For example, if your friend is telling you about a movie she saw, you do not need to summarize what she says.

Practice

Practice good listening skills with a partner. One of you can play the part of Angelo, and one can play Larry. Angelo will start by saying, "I really messed up today." Larry will be a good listener. He will follow the skills for good listening on pages 43–45. After the conversation, discuss what Larry did to show he was listening.

Body language often reveals a person's true feelings.

4-3 ▸ Talking Without Words

The words people say can tell you a lot. However, **body language** can tell you even more. Body language is showing feelings using your body and your face. It includes tapping your toes and crossing your arms. It also includes a smile or raised eyebrows.

You can tell right away how some of the students in the picture on page 45 feel. They do not have to say a word. They are showing their feelings with their bodies and their faces.

Sometimes body language is not clear. The same body language can have two or more meanings. For example, a tapping toe can mean someone is angry. It can also mean someone is in a hurry. Raised eyebrows can show surprise or disbelief.

Practice

With a partner, make up a short scene to show how body language can communicate meaning. For example, one partner could read a letter. He or she could use body language to show whether the letter is happy, sad, or surprising. The listener's body language could show whether he or she is a friend, an enemy, or a stranger.

Present your scene to other students. Afterward, ask them what you communicated using body language.

4-4 ▸ Avoiding Confusing Messages

Think About It

You confuse people when your words say one thing but your body language says another. What can you do about that?

You are talking to a friend. You tell him you cannot go to the movies with him tonight. He says, "That's okay. No problem." However, now he will not look at you. His body seems stiff. He is giving you a confusing message. His body language says he is very angry. However, his words say he is not angry.

Listeners may pay more attention to body language than to words because body language often shows true feelings. When people talk, they may try to hide these feelings. However, their body language gives them away.

If you are angry, you need to express those feelings in words. Do not try to hide them. Your body language will tell others your feelings anyway. It is often better to tell others you are angry rather than making the problem worse by trying to hide your feelings.

Practice

Think of something to tell a partner, such as "I would be glad to come to your party." As you say the words, show a different feeling with your body language. For example, you might frown as you say you are glad. Talk about how these confusing messages make communication more difficult.

4-5 Communicating in Different Cultures

You learned to talk by listening to your family members talk. You learned to use body language the same way, by watching the people around you. You saw their faces when they were surprised. Then you made your face look like theirs.

If you had grown up in Japan, Saudi Arabia, Brazil, or Congo, you would have learned different words. You might have also learned different body language.

It is important to remember that the way people from another country communicate may be very different from what you are used to. When you speak with someone from another country, try to understand and respect those differences. For example, Olga met Yoko, the Japanese exchange student at her school. Olga smiled and looked directly at Yoko. "How do you like our school so far?" Olga asked. Olga noticed that when

Did You Know

In some cultures, looking away from a person who is speaking is a way to show respect.

she talked to Yoko, Yoko did not look at her. Yoko looked down at the floor. Olga thought Yoko was bored or was not interested in talking with her. Olga also noticed that Yoko seemed uncomfortable when she answered Olga's question. Then their teacher explained that in Japan, looking down was sometimes a sign of respect, while looking at the speaker's face was sometimes a sign of a lack of respect.

Roger was confused when he met Hakeem at a friend's house. Hakeem's family was visiting from Saudi Arabia. When Roger started talking to him, Hakeem moved very close to him. This made Roger feel uncomfortable. Roger stopped talking and took a few steps backward. When he started talking again, Hakeem moved closer to him. He wondered if Hakeem was trying to annoy him. He seemed friendly enough.

▶ **Everyday Tip**
Do not judge a new friend too harshly. Give yourself time to get to know him or her before you form your opinion.

Later, Roger asked his friend why Hakeem moved so close when they spoke. Roger's friend explained that in Hakeem's culture, moving closer to a speaker showed interest in what he or she was saying.

Of course, different ways of communicating can lead to misunderstandings. Olga thought Yoko was not interested in talking with her. Roger thought Hakeem might be trying to annoy him.

Sometimes people do not communicate in the way we expect. If this happens, we should not judge them so quickly. Like Olga and Roger, we might find that these new friends express themselves in different ways than we do.

The Golden Rule of Communicating
Good communicators listen to other people the same way they want others to listen to them. This is called the Golden Rule. Treat others the way that you want to be treated. This is a good rule not only for communicating, but for living. Work to understand what is being said and what people are feeling.

Read the conversation below between Carrie and April. Then follow the steps to help Carrie decide what to do.

Carrie: "When I get home today, I need to call..."

April: "You need to call your mom at work, right? Why are you telling me that, Carrie? I know you call her every day."

Carrie: "No, I need to call the library and..."

April: "And see if it has that new CD, right? If you get it, I want to hear it, too."

Carrie: "April! Let me finish! I need to call the library and see when it closes today."

On a separate sheet of paper, follow the steps below to help Carrie decide what to do about April.

STEP 1 Identify the decision Carrie must make.

STEP 2 List Carrie's choices.

STEP 3 Cross out any choices that are harmful or might be against Carrie's beliefs.

STEP 4 Think about the possible results of the remaining choices.

STEP 5 Select the best choice.

STEP 6 Explain how Carrie would carry out that choice.

STEP 7 Describe the possible results of Carrie's choice.

Make a Difference
If you could give Carrie advice, what would you tell her to do if April keeps interrupting her?

Chapter

4 ▷ Review

Summary

Poor listeners can discourage speakers from talking. They do this by interrupting, giving advice, and telling their own stories instead of listening.

Good listeners encourage speakers to talk. They do this by paying attention, letting the speaker talk, and asking questions. They also listen for the feelings of the speaker and summarize what the speaker has said.

People also communicate with body language. Sometimes body language says one thing, but words say another. This can be confusing for listeners.

Our families teach us how to communicate. People from different cultures sometimes communicate in different ways.

Good communicators are thoughtful of others. They communicate with other people in the same way that they want others to communicate with them.

Vocabulary Review

express

summarize

advice

body language

communicate

Complete each sentence with a term from the list. Use a separate sheet of paper.

1. When people _____ , they share their thoughts, feelings, or ideas with others.

2. A suggestion about what should be done is called _____ .

3. To _____ means to show your thoughts, feelings, or ideas.

4. To explain the main ideas of what you heard, saw, or read is to _____ .

5. When you show feelings using your body and your face, you are using _____ .

Chapter Quiz

Write your answers in complete sentences.

1. What are three ways a listener might discourage a speaker from talking?

2. Every time Jason talks to Kurt, Kurt tries to tell him what to do. What is Kurt doing that makes him a poor listener?

3. What are five ways to encourage a speaker to talk?

4. When Sara talks to Brooke, she knows Brooke is listening. What are some specific things Brooke might be doing to show Sara that she is listening?

5. What are two kinds of body language?

6. You can tell a friend is sad by looking at him or her. What body language might tell you that your friend is sad?

7. **CRITICAL THINKING** How can different ways of communicating lead to misunderstandings?

Writing Activity

On a separate sheet of paper, write a paragraph to describe how you feel when someone is not listening to you.

Group Activity

Read the listening skills on pages 43 to 45. With a partner, take turns practicing good listening skills. Afterward, write down what worked best. Then share with the class what you did to be good listeners.

When people know how to work together, they can accomplish almost anything. What are some things you can accomplish that would be hard to do working alone?

Learning Objectives

- Explain how different needs and points of view can cause conflicts.

- Explain "I messages."

- Demonstrate how to show confidence and respect as you talk with others.

- Describe ways to cool off angry feelings.

- Explain how people's thoughts can lead to angry feelings.

- List the steps in settling conflicts.

Chapter 5 Getting Along With Others

Words to Know

opinion	a belief
point of view	a way of thinking about something
conflict	a strong disagreement caused by a difference in needs or points of view

In the situation below, Adam and Christa are having an argument. Decide whether that means they have to stop being friends.

Adam and Christa are talking about an idea that might become a law. The law would stop lumber companies from cutting down the forests near their town. "What about the birds and animals that live in the forest?" Adam asks Christa. "Where are they supposed to live?"

"Most of them will move to another part of the forest," Christa tells him. "Anyway, the lumber companies always plant trees in place of the ones they cut."

"The trees they plant are tiny! It will take forever for them to grow," Adam says. "But the lumber companies don't care about that! All they care about is making money!"

Christa gives Adam an angry look and walks away. Adam does not know that Christa's parents work for a lumber company. If the law is passed, her mom and dad might lose their jobs. Christa doesn't know that Adam has a part-time job taking care of injured wild animals.

Christa does not share Adam's **opinion,** or belief, about the law that would stop lumber companies from cutting down the forests. Christa has a different **point of view,** or way of thinking, about the issue than Adam. Adam is concerned about the animals. He wants the companies to stop chopping down the forests. Christa also cares about the animals and the forests. However, she is more worried about her parents' jobs. She wants to let the lumber companies cut down the forests. She knows that the companies will replace the trees they cut.

It is all right for Adam and Christa to have different points of view. This is bound to happen because they have different interests and needs. However, their different points of view are keeping them from getting along. Christa is angry with Adam for putting down the lumber companies. Adam thinks Christa does not care about the animals.

Better communication may not make this problem go away. People will always disagree about certain issues. Christa and Adam may continue to disagree about cutting down the forests. Still, better communication could help them get along and stay friends.

Right now, Adam and Christa see only part of the picture. They both need to see the whole picture. They need to understand each other's point of view. Then they might not feel so angry with each other.

If Adam knew about Christa's parents, he might feel differently. Then he would understand why she defends the lumber companies. If Christa knew about Adam's part-time job, she might think differently. Then she would understand why he cares so much about saving the forests.

Did You Know ?

Knowing just your own point of view is like listening to someone talking on the telephone. If you hear only one person speaking, you hear only part of the story.

Practice

With a partner, role-play a conflict between two friends who disagree about something.

5-2   Understanding Causes of Conflicts

Conflict is a part of life. It is a strong disagreement caused by a difference in people's needs or points of view.

Simon and Megan are brother and sister. Both of them have household jobs to do. They take turns setting and clearing the dinner table and washing the dishes. When Simon sets and clears the table, Megan washes the dishes. The next day, they switch jobs.

Yesterday, Simon was not home for dinner. He ate dinner at a friend's house. Megan had to set and clear the table and wash the dishes. Tonight, Megan tells Simon she needs to work on her science project. That means Simon will have to do both jobs. Simon says he does not think that is fair. He will not have time to practice his lines for the school play.

This difference in needs is causing a conflict. Megan and Simon have to find a solution they can agree on.

In some conflicts, people might never agree. Like Adam and Christa, they may look at a problem from different points of view. They need to try to understand each other's point of view. They might still have a conflict. However, they might be able to work out a solution. They could get along better with each other.

People often have conflicts because of different points of view. Suppose a school system has to cut back on its programs. Philip, who plays basketball, thinks the swim team should be cut. Juan is on the swim team. He thinks the basketball program should be cut. Neither is right or wrong. They just have different opinions. They need to try to understand each other's

Think About It

The next time you have a conflict with someone, think about the cause. Do you have different points of view?

point of view. Then they could still be friends. They might even work together to think of other ways for the school to save money.

Practice

Young people and their families sometimes have different points of view. Choose one of the topics below. Explain a young person's point of view. Then explain an older family member's point of view. Describe how explaining their points of view to each other might help them get along.

Topics		
curfews	haircuts	homework
using the car	using the telephone	watching television
clothes	dating	allowances

5-3 ▸ Using "I Messages"

Sometimes conflicts lead to arguments and hard feelings. Think back to the conflict between Philip and Juan. Suppose Philip and Juan are talking about which school program should be cut. Philip might remind Juan that the swim team lost the city championship. Philip defends his point of view by saying the swimmers are losers. They should not get any school funds. Then Juan gets angry. He points out that Philip missed two shots at the last basketball game. Juan says the team lost the game because of Philip.

Juan and Philip are ready to fight. Yet, they could explain their feelings about the school cuts in ways that will not lead to a fight. They could use "I messages." "I messages" can help people of all ages explain to others how they feel. "I messages" have three parts.

1. I feel… (describe how you feel, such as angry, embarrassed, or worried)

2. when you… (explain what is bothering you)

3. because… (tell why this bothers you)

In an "I message," you do not have to say the exact words, "I feel… when you… because…." You can use different words. Just explain how you feel, and why.

Here are some examples of "I messages."

> "I feel angry when you put down the swim team, because we work hard."

> "I feel embarrassed when you blame me for losing the game. I didn't mean to miss those shots."

> "It worries me that the school might cut the swimming program. Next year we have a good chance to win the championship."

Avoiding Attacking Messages

Be careful not to attack the other person when explaining your feelings. An attack can lead to hard feelings.

The two messages below show the difference between an "I message" and an "attacking message." Jim and Chris share a locker at school. Which message do you think Jim would want to hear?

I Message

"I feel frustrated when I try to find things in our locker. I was late for my math class again today because I couldn't find my book."

Attacking Message

"You are such a pig! Why do you throw all your garbage in our locker? I can't find anything in this mess!"

Remember
Treat others the way that you want to be treated. Work to understand what people are feeling.

If Chris gave Jim the first message, Jim might be willing to clean out the locker. This message explains the problem without blaming anyone. But if Chris gave Jim the second message, Jim might not be so willing to help. The "attacking message" blames Jim for the problem. It even calls Jim names. Jim might be angry and hurt.

"I messages" take some practice. But they are worth the effort. They can prevent some conflicts and angry feelings. They can also help solve conflicts. They do this by allowing people to explain their points of view without insulting each other. You can use "I messages" to show that you respect, or value, someone's opinion even if you do not agree with it. In this way, "I messages" help us understand others and get along.

Practice

Write an "I message" to each person below. Use a separate sheet of paper.

1. Your younger brother lost your keys.

2. A friend told people a secret about you.

3. Your mother never knocks on the door before coming into your bedroom.

5-4 ▶ Communicating With Confidence

Do not waste "I messages" by saying one thing with your words and another with your body language. For example, Hope was upset. Her friend Lisa kept interrupting her. "I feel angry when you keep interrupting me, Lisa. I have something important to tell you," Hope whispered as she looked at the floor.

"What did you say, Hope?" Lisa asked.

"Never mind," Hope said quickly.

Use good body language to show you are a confident speaker.

Hope's body language made her "I message" weak. Hope should have looked Lisa in the eye. She could have said the same words, but in a clear, confident voice. Lisa would have heard her more easily. Then Lisa might have stopped interrupting her.

Practice

Have a partner listen as you say each sentence below. Say the sentence once as if you are not sure of yourself. Then say the sentence with confidence. Discuss the differences between the statements when they are said differently.

1. Would you wait for me after school?

2. I feel left out because you went to the movies without me. I like to go to the movies with you.

3. I want to draw the pictures for our project.

Some people always say what they are thinking, even if they insult someone. Some people often use a loud voice. Others use attacking messages. This is not part of good communication.

Lisa's friend Hope did not speak up when Lisa interrupted her. However, Lisa also has a friend named Molly. Once Lisa interrupted Molly. Molly frowned and put her hands on her hips. She said, "Lisa, you loudmouth, I was talking! You interrupted me! Wait until I'm finished!"

Molly does not care about other people's feelings. She often insists that everyone do things her way. It can be hard to get this type of person to listen to your ideas.

▶ **Everyday Tip**
Use a calm, clear voice when you are communicating. Your tone of voice is an important part of your message.

Good communication comes from respect. Speaking with confidence shows that you respect yourself. By avoiding attacking messages, you show that you respect other people.

Another way to show that you respect yourself and others is to stand or sit up straight when you talk. Look the other person in the eye when communicating. It is also important to speak in a calm, clear voice—no whispering and no shouting.

Show that you respect others by using good listening skills. Do not put others down. Explain your own ideas without insulting theirs. Consider others' opinions, but make your own decisions.

Dealing With Angry Feelings

Suppose you used an "I message" to ask someone not to interrupt you. However, the person kept doing it. When others do not treat us with respect, angry thoughts come into our heads. Sometimes, a person might say or do something that he or she will be sorry about later.

Try to be aware of these angry feelings. If this happens, then you can deal with these feelings before they get out of control. Use tricks to calm down. Count to ten—or even twenty. Counting gives you time to calm down. Another trick is to take two or three deep breaths. This will help you relax.

If you are very angry, explain that you want to talk about this problem later. In the meantime, calm down by thinking calm thoughts. You could also discuss the problem with someone else. Find a good listener. A good listener might be able to help you figure out a way to solve the problem.

Remember
Sometimes our body language says one thing, but our words say another.

Sometimes by getting exercise, you calm down. You can overcome feelings of anger by being physically active. Take a walk, ride your bike, clean your room. It might get your mind off the problem or give you time to think it through.

Practice

How can you tell that a person is getting angry? Does the person's face get red? Does the person frown? Make a list of at least four signs of anger.

5-6 Avoiding Anger

Sometimes people make themselves angry. They may make themselves angry by the way they think about something they see.

Suppose you see a girl laughing in the hallway. You could think that she just heard a joke. You could also think that she is making fun of you. This second thought could make you angry, even though it might not be true.

Read the chart on page 62. The sentences on the left show some thoughts that can lead to angry feelings. The sentences on the right can lead to calm feelings.

Angry Thoughts	Calm Thoughts
I'll never learn this!	It will take time for me to learn this.
He'll be sorry he said that!	I will not let him bother me.
She is not my boss!	I can make my own decisions.
He lied to me!	I don't think he said that yesterday.
She broke it on purpose!	I'll ask her to buy me a new one.

If you start to feel angry, your thoughts might be the problem. If you change your thoughts, you might feel calmer. More importantly, you will be able to think more clearly. Feeling calm and thinking clearly will help you get along with other people.

Practice

Think of calm thoughts to finish these sentences. Write an ending to each sentence on a separate sheet of paper.

1. Lee lost my newest CD, but...

2. Aunt Lisa will not let me get my driver's license, but...

3. Dom likes someone else better than he likes me, but...

5-7 ▸ Finding Methods of Settling Conflicts

If you are having trouble settling a conflict, calm down before you speak. If you feel angry, you may say things you do not mean. Remember to listen carefully. Invite the other person to explain the conflict from his or her point of view.

By explaining your point of view you might be able to think of ways to settle the conflict. Both of you should list as many possible solutions as you can.

The more choices you have, the better chance you have of finding one you both like. Then discuss the choices. Cross out any that either person does not like.

Finally, choose the best solution for both of you. Try to choose a solution that helps both people. That way, neither one of you will feel angry or cheated.

Solving Conflicts

Doug just spent two hours helping JB study for a test. Doug works as a tutor and he expected JB to pay him for his help. JB thought Doug was helping him as a friend. He does not have any money to pay Doug. Both are very upset about the misunderstanding.

Doug and JB used the methods mentioned above to settle their conflict. Doug took several deep breaths to let out his anger, while JB walked to the kitchen to get a drink of water. They both gave themselves time to cool off.

Then Doug asked why JB thought Doug's help would be free. Doug listened quietly as JB explained that since they

▶ **Everyday Tip**
Conflicts can be very upsetting. Take time to calm down. This is the first step to solving a problem.

The best way to settle a conflict is to talk calmly about the situation.

had been friends for a long time, he thought the tutoring was a simple favor. JB also admitted that he was broke.

Doug then explained his point of view. He calmly told JB, "I feel angry because you didn't plan to pay me. I am saving all the money I make for college. I need every cent."

▶ **Everyday Tip**
Listen to the other person's point of view. It is always helpful.

Once Doug and JB explained their points of view, they began to think of ways to settle the conflict. Doug and JB listed ways to solve their conflict.

1. JB pays Doug nothing.

2. JB pays Doug what he usually earns for two hours of tutoring.

3. JB pays part of Doug's fee now and the rest later.

4. JB repays Doug by baby-sitting Doug's little brother for two afternoons. That would give Doug more time to tutor other students.

After discussing their choices, Doug crossed out Choice 1. JB will not have any money for a while, so he crossed out Choices 2 and 3. To settle their conflict they must choose the best solution for both. Doug agreed to have JB baby-sit his little brother. In fact, the two friends decided to trade more tutoring for baby-sitting.

Whenever people work or play together, they have conflicts. Yet conflicts do not have to lead to angry feelings. They also do not have to break up friendships. For example, Doug and JB found a way to settle their conflict in a way that helped both of them.

Practice

Think about the last time you and your best friend had a conflict. How did you solve the conflict? Write a paragraph describing the conflict and how you solved it.

YOU DECIDE
Ways to Solve a Conflict

Read the situation below. Then follow the steps to help Alice decide what to do.

Alice is angry at Pamela, but she cannot decide what to do. Nearly every day at lunch time, Pamela asks for part of Alice's lunch. Sometimes Pamela wants half of Alice's sandwich. Other times, she reaches over and takes one of Alice's cookies.

Alice knows that some conflicts are not important enough to bring up. But conflicts can grow if you ignore them.

On a separate sheet of paper, follow the steps below to help Alice decide what to do.

STEP 1   Identify the decision Alice must make.

STEP 2   List Alice's choices.

STEP 3   Cross out any choices that are harmful or might go against Alice's beliefs.

STEP 4   Think about the possible results of the remaining choices.

STEP 5   Select the best choice.

STEP 6   Explain how Alice would carry out that choice.

STEP 7   Describe the possible results of Alice's choice.

Make a Difference
What would you advise Alice to do next time Pamela takes part of her lunch?

Chapter

5 / Review

Summary

Conflicts often result when people have different needs or points of view. Understanding others' needs or points of view can often lead to solving a conflict.
"I messages" explain what is bothering you without attacking the other person. "I messages" can help settle conflicts.
Some conflicts are caused by not telling people when they are bothering you. Other conflicts are caused by attacking people when they bother you.
You can avoid some conflicts by explaining your opinions with confidence. Look the other person in the eye and speak calmly and politely. Use good listening skills. Do not put down others.
Angry feelings can make a conflict worse. You can cool off by counting to ten, taking deep breaths, or asking for time to calm down. You can also discuss the problem with someone else or get some exercise.
What you tell yourself about a situation makes a difference. If you tell yourself something negative, you can make yourself feel angry. If you tell yourself something positive, you can help yourself feel calm.
To settle a conflict, listen to each other's point of view. Then work together to think of ways to settle the problem. Choose a way that you agree on peacefully.

Vocabulary Review

conflict
opinion
point of view

Match each definition with the correct term from the list. Use a separate sheet of paper.

1. a way of thinking about something
2. a belief
3. a strong disagreement caused by a difference in needs or points of view

Chapter Quiz

Write your answers in complete sentences.

1. What are the three parts of an "I message"?

2. Jenny looks at the floor and whispers, "I'm sorry, Carrie, but don't take my book without telling me." How could Jenny make her point in a better way?

3. Carrie yells at Jenny, "I didn't take your dumb book!" How could Carrie show Jenny more respect?

4. What are three ways to calm down if you are feeling angry?

5. Glen was not chosen for the soccer team. "I can try again next season," he tells himself. How would this thought make Glen feel?

6. What are the steps you should follow to settle a conflict?

7. **CRITICAL THINKING** What is your point of view about having a dress code at school? What is a different point of view about this?

Writing Activity

Some people think conflict is bad. They avoid conflict by letting others have their own way. They say nothing when someone or something is bothering them. On a separate sheet of paper, explain whether you think people should try to avoid conflict in this way, and why.

Group Activity

Think of a conflict you or someone you know had with someone else. Describe it to a small group. If the conflict was settled, explain how. If the conflict was not settled, explain why not. With your group, role-play one other solution to the conflict.

People go through many changes, such as moving into a new home. Change can sometimes cause stress and confusion. How can working together make the stress of change easier?

Learning Objectives

- Describe changes that take place during teenage years.
- Explain how changes can affect teenagers.
- Describe ways teenagers can deal with change.
- Explain how teenagers' relationships with their families can change.
- Describe how changes in the community can affect teenagers.
- Identify some ways to reduce stress.

Chapter 6 — Handling Change and Stress

Words to Know

stress	uncomfortable feelings caused when you have too much to deal with
mature	adult
hormones	chemicals in your body that cause and help control physical changes
emotions	feelings

Julie feels confused. Here is what different people told her, all in the same day.

> In the morning, Julie's older brother told her, "No, you can't ride to school with me and my friends. We don't want any little kids around."
>
> Then her father reminded her, "Don't forget to go to Grandpa's house and check on him after school, Julie. He might need your help. You know he depends on you."
>
> At school, her best friend said, "Your parents won't let you go out with Robbie? They really treat you like a baby, Julie. They should start letting you make your own decisions!"

6-1 Understanding Change and Stress

Julie is getting confusing messages. She is expected to act like an adult but is often treated like a child. Julie wants to make more of her own decisions. Yet she has no idea what to do with the rest of her life.

Nothing seems to stay the same. Like other young people, suddenly she has to deal with all kinds of changes within herself, her family, and her community.

Some of the changes she is experiencing can cause **stress.** Stress is the uncomfortable feelings caused when you have too much to deal with. This chapter includes suggestions that can help you deal with stress.

Practice

Start thinking about the changes going on in your life. On a separate sheet of paper, list the following.

- ways you are changing

- ways your family is changing

- ways your community is changing

Save this list for yourself. You might want to add to it after you finish the chapter.

6-2 ▸ Understanding Changes Within Yourself

▶ **Everyday Tip**
Even when the outside of your body is changing, you are the same person on the inside.

Physical changes are some of the major changes people face in their lives. As children become teenagers, they get taller, wider, rounder, and stronger. They even get hairier. Their bodies become **mature**, or adult. **Hormones** are the chemicals in your body that cause and help control these changes.

Everybody develops at a different speed. Some teenagers develop a little more quickly than others. Some develop a little more slowly.

This means that teenagers often end up looking different from their friends for a while. Looking different can feel uncomfortable. It can be harder to deal with than the changes themselves. Still, by the age of 16 or 17, the slow developers have often caught up with the quick ones. By then, most of the physical changes are over.

Nevertheless, teenagers need time to get used to their new bodies. Growing four to six inches in a year does take some getting used to.

The same hormones that help your body become adult also affect your **emotions,** or feelings. Sometimes they send your emotions on a roller coaster ride. Julie says she feels like smiling one minute and crying the next. Her emotional ups and downs confuse her family. At times they even confuse Julie.

Her friend Robbie is having trouble controlling his temper. He gets mad about things that never used to bother him. Other times he feels like crying or says things he does not mean.

All these emotional changes can make it harder to get along with others. It helps to understand that these changes are just part of becoming an adult. Remember, the hormones that cause physical changes can also affect moods and feelings. In time, emotions do become easier to manage.

> **Did You Know ?**
> The fact that people look and act differently adds to the variety of the world. Our differences make each of us special.

With all these physical and emotional changes, many teenagers worry about being "normal." If other young people like them, they think they must be normal. If other teenagers ignore or tease them, they may feel "different" and unlovable. It is important not to let others' judgments of you affect how you feel.

Practice

Write the answers to these questions on a separate sheet of paper.

1. In what ways do teenagers try to look and act like other teenagers?

2. What problems can be caused by the emotional changes teenagers go through?

Having friends is important, especially for teenagers and young adults. Doing things with friends helps you learn how to get along with people. Friends listen when you want to talk about problems. They can help you feel good about yourself.

Some young people are scared of looking or acting different from their friends. They want to be just like everyone else. They think that this way they will be accepted by other young people and have many friends.

These young people may be willing to do almost anything to be part of a group. They may let a group tell them what to do. They should be learning to make their own decisions. Young people may find that making a decision that goes against their group causes them to lose friends.

As people grow and change, their friendships often change as well.

However, friends may come and go. When some people lose a friend, they think it means no one likes them. It usually just means that they or their friends have changed.

For example, Rick, Ramón, and Tony were best friends when they were younger. They spent hours together making and launching model rockets. Now Rick has band practice after school. He often goes away on band trips. Ramón runs track and hangs around with guys on the track team. Tony has a new girlfriend. She takes up lots of his time. Rick, Ramón, and Tony do not spend much time with one another anymore. They are no longer best friends because their interests have changed.

People often grow closer to some friends as their interests change. Rick was always friends with Greg. However, now Greg is his best friend. They both enjoy playing in the band. They discovered they also share other interests.

As young people get older, their thinking patterns change in ways that help them plan for the future and solve problems. This allows them to consider their choices. They can make wiser decisions. In time, young people tend to become more aware of other people's feelings. They try not to do or say things that may hurt others' feelings. These changes in thinking patterns are just another part of becoming an adult.

Practice

On a separate sheet of paper, list at least five things you liked to do when you were much younger. Then list five things you like to do now. What do the lists tell you about how your interests have changed?

6-4 ▸ Understanding Changes Within a Family

Families are important in helping children grow and become independent. However, families often change. Parents may have or adopt other children.

Older children may move out of the home. Married brothers or sisters may have children of their own. Grandparents and other relatives may move in—or out.

Think About It

What are some family changes that cause stress for teenagers?

Divorce is another big change that affects many families. As a result, many children and teenagers live with just one parent. Some live with one parent part of the time and the other parent the rest of the time. When the parents remain friends, living in two homes can work out fairly well. When the parents feel angry with each other, living in two homes can be difficult. Then their children are more likely to feel angry, too. Their children may also worry about their future.

When two divorced adults marry each other, their children may live together as one family. Sometimes these parents have another child together. The relationships among the members of these families can be warm and loving. Yet sometimes they are tense. Talking about your feelings and problems with family members can help.

Families, Money, and Moving
Families face many kinds of changes when a member has a serious illness or accident. Sometimes disease or injury may cause the death of a family member. This is upsetting for children and teenagers in the family.

Having less money can also cause stress in a family. A family may have less income if a parent becomes too ill to work. Some parents lose their jobs when their companies close or decide they do not need as many employees. Divorce can also change a family's income level. When parents have to pay for two separate homes, they have less money for other things.

Of course, a family's income can also increase. A parent may get a raise, or an older child may begin working. Gaining more income, however, usually does not cause as much stress as losing income.

A divorce, new job, or job transfer may cause a family to move. Some families decide to move closer to a sick relative. Or a family member's health problems may require a warmer climate. Whatever the reason, a move can affect nearly every part of a young person's life.

When a family changes, routines change. For example, if a parent takes on a second job, the family's daily schedule may be upset. Family members may no longer be able to spend time together.

Teenagers may be expected to take on more responsibilities. For example, they might have to care for younger children or cook meals. If they can drive, they might become the family taxi. One afternoon, they might have to take a brother to soccer practice. The next day, they might be asked to drive a cousin to the doctor.

With so much going on, young family members might not be able to find a good listener when they need one. An older brother or sister may move out. Or a parent or grandparent may not be there.

In the meantime, teenagers must still go to school, work, do homework, attend sports practices, and so on. They must also deal with all the normal changes that are happening within themselves.

Family changes can cause uncomfortable feelings. It is normal to feel angry, scared, or upset by family changes. Some young people become angry with a grandparent for getting so sick. They may be upset about having to help out so much at home. They need help themselves. Learning to cope with these feelings can help ease the stress during times of change.

Using Technology

Computer software sometimes has a calendar feature. Using it can help you manage your time and responsibilities.

Practice

Think about your family or the family of someone you know. Write how the changes mentioned in this section make you or this other person feel.

Handling Family Changes

There are ways to help you deal with the stress of family changes. Accept changes that you cannot do anything about. You cannot stop people from getting a divorce. However, you can work to keep a good relationship with your parents. Remember that their divorce is not your fault. If a family member has a serious illness, try to cheer up the person or offer comfort. You cannot cure him or her, but you can try to help. Change is a normal part of life. Try to deal positively with unwanted change.

A family may have many needs during a change. However, young people cannot meet all of their family's needs. If someone asks you to do more than you can do, try using "I messages" to explain how you feel. Or ask another family member to help you talk with your parent or parents. Accepting too much responsibility can cause stress. It might even hurt your health. That will not help anyone.

Nearly every change has its good points. For example, if your grandmother moves in, you might be able to learn more about your family history. If you write down her stories, you can share them with the rest of the family.

If someone in your family is ill, you can learn about the illness. Find out what kinds of help are available. Gaining knowledge about a problem can teach you how to handle other problems in the future.

Other Kinds of Family Changes

All families change, even if no one moves into the home or gets sick. As teenagers get older, their relationships with their parents change. Young people want to make more of their own decisions. They want their families to give them more freedom and set fewer rules.

Yet some young people are not ready to make wise decisions. For example, Joanna asked her parents to give her money every Monday to buy lunches at school.

Think About It

Do you think this is good advice? Why or why not?

- Accept the things you cannot change.
- Change the things you can.
- Think carefully so you will know the difference.

However, Joanna decided to spend her lunch money on CDs. Since she did not eat lunch, she had no energy in the afternoons. Joanna began falling asleep in her classes. By the time she got home from school, she was starving and grouchy. Her grades fell as well.

Joanna's parents may still need to help her make decisions. However, other families may make too many decisions for their children. They may not realize that their children are maturing.

For example, Pete's mother still picks out his shirts. She buys styles that no one at school wears. When Pete does not wear these shirts, his mother becomes angry. Talking calmly with his mother about the problem and asking her to talk to other mothers might help. If Pete is respectful, his mother might realize that it is time to give Pete more responsibility.

Changing relationships between teenagers and parents can cause stress. To handle these changes, everyone needs patience and good listening skills.

Did You Know

It can be difficult for parents to know when children should have more freedom to make their own decisions. A young person can help by showing responsibility.

Practice

On a separate sheet of paper, list three family changes that someone might face. Next to each change, write how you would handle the change.

6-6 Handling Community Changes

Some communities have not changed much over the past 50 or 60 years. Others change every month. In these changing communities, houses might be built, or apartment buildings might be torn down. People might move into or out of an area. New factories might be set up, or companies might go out of business.

When a business moves into a community, it usually hires new employees. More people may move into the community to take those jobs. With more customers available, new stores may open.

However, when a business closes, its employees lose their jobs. They may have to move to another city or state to find work. There will be fewer people in the community. Stores, shops, and movie theaters will have fewer customers. They may have to close, too.

If you live in a changing community, you might see changes at your school. A community that is losing families is also losing students. It might have to close a nearly empty school and send those students to another school. The students will have to get used to new teachers, new friends, and new rules. This can be very stressful for the students.

Schools in a growing community may have too many students. Some classes might have to be held in the gym or library. Noise and confusion could make it hard to concentrate.

Many of the tips for dealing with the stress of family changes can also help you deal with changes in your community. For example, if your school is closed, look on the bright side of going to a new school. You will have the chance to meet new people and make new friends. Some of these new friendships may last a lifetime.

Practice

Suppose some of the changes mentioned in this section affected your community. On a separate sheet of paper, write about how you think the changes should be handled.

Everyone experiences some stress. A little stress is good for you. It gives you energy and helps you do your best. Still, too much stress can make you sick. Below is a chart of some signs of too much stress.

Signs of Too Much Stress	
frequent illnesses	teeth grinding
nail biting	lack of patience
headaches and other pains	sleeping problems
tight muscles	tiredness
problems in getting along with others	

If you have some of these signs of stress, you might be dealing with some kind of change. However, change is not the only cause of stress.

Young adulthood can be stressful. Activities like sports can lower stress levels before they cause problems.

Expecting too much of yourself also causes stress. People who always expect to win are under a great deal of stress. They need to find other ways to feel good about themselves. For example, they might learn how to play a musical instrument. Then winning will be less important. Losing will cause less stress.

Some people are always hurrying. Managing their time will cut down on this stress. With some planning, they will be able to get important tasks done. They will also have more time to enjoy life.

Wanting to fit in causes some teenagers to worry about whether others like them. To avoid this stress, they should find friends who accept them as they are. They will feel comfortable with these friends. Then they can relax and be themselves.

Conflicts with parents, teachers, friends, and others can cause stress. Teenagers may feel angry, guilty, or just uncomfortable about these conflicts. They need to learn how to settle arguments peacefully. Then they can cut down on this source of stress.

A balanced diet can help your body deal with stress. Instead of eating junk food and sugar, eat more fresh fruits and vegetables. They give your body what it needs to repair body parts that get worn out by stress.

Exercise strengthens your muscles, especially your heart. Exercise also works off that extra energy that builds up when you are angry and stressed. A strong, relaxed body is better able to deal with stress.

No one can escape change or stress. They are part of life. However, being able to handle change and stress is a sign that you are ready to live independently.

Using Technology

Consider using a word processing program to keep a journal. Sometimes writing about situations helps resolve conflicts.

Practice

What are five ways to deal with stress? Write your list on a separate sheet of paper.

Read the situation below. Then follow the steps to wise decision-making to help Duane decide what to do.

Duane's relatives always eat dinner together on Thanksgiving. However, this Thanksgiving, Duane's hiking club will have its first trip. The group will leave Thanksgiving morning and return on Sunday. Duane's best friends are going on the trip. This would also be his chance to go on a long hiking trip. At the same time, Duane's Aunt Sarah will be driving 300 miles to be with the family at Thanksgiving. He has not seen her for a year.

On a separate sheet of paper, follow the steps below to help Duane decide what to do.

STEP 1   Identify the decision Duane must make.

STEP 2   List Duane's choices.

STEP 3   Cross out any choices that are harmful or might be against Duane's beliefs.

STEP 4   Think about the possible results of the remaining choices.

STEP 5   Select the best choice.

STEP 6   Explain how Duane would carry out that choice.

STEP 7   Describe the possible results of Duane's choice.

Make a Difference

If you could give Duane advice, what would you tell him about going on the hiking trip?

Summary

Teenagers face physical, emotional, social, and mental changes. These changes can be confusing. Still, they are normal and natural.
Families also face changes. They may gain or lose members. Family members may have health problems or lose their jobs.
Young people can deal with family changes by accepting them. They should set limits on how much they can help their families.
Many teenagers want to make their own decisions. However, they need to be responsible first. Parents need to realize when young people are ready to make decisions.
A community might change by gaining or losing residents. These changes may affect local jobs and school conditions.
Causes of stress include dealing with change, expecting too much of yourself, and hurrying. Other causes are wanting to fit in and arguing with others. Eating the wrong foods and not exercising can make stress worse.
To handle stress, you should be realistic about what you can do. Plan your time and find friends with whom you feel comfortable. Eating right and exercising can also help.

Vocabulary Review

Write *true* or *false* after each sentence. If the sentence is false, change the underlined word to make it true. Use a separate sheet of paper.

1. When you show your <u>emotions</u>, you are showing your feelings.

2. <u>Hormones</u> means uncomfortable feelings caused when you have too much to deal with.

3. A teenager's body is becoming <u>mature</u>.

4. <u>Stress</u> means chemicals in your body that cause and help control physical changes.

Chapter Quiz

Write your answers in complete sentences.

1. What are three physical changes teenagers face?

2. What are three causes of stress?

3. What are three ways to reduce stress?

4. Why is a 16-year-old usually better at solving problems than a 6-year-old?

5. Bernard keeps cutting classes. He cannot understand why his parents will not let him stay out later on weekends. Why do you think Bernard's parents are so strict about when he should be home?

6. Why does belonging to a group keep some young people from learning how to make wise decisions?

7. **CRITICAL THINKING** A big company is building a factory in your town. How might this factory affect you, even if you do not work there?

Writing Activity

Kathleen is 16 years old and wants to get her driver's license. However, her parents want her to wait another year. Kathleen wants to show her parents she is responsible enough to get her license. On a separate sheet of paper, write a paragraph describing what Kathleen could do to show responsibility.

Group Activity

Suppose your uncle moves in with your family. He takes your room, and you have to share a room with your sister or brother. In a small group, role-play how you feel and how you will handle this change. Then write the scene. Include words that describe your feelings.

Unit 2 **Review**

Read each sentence below. Then choose the letter that best completes each one.

1. A true friend
   A. likes you for yourself.
   B. respects the things you think are important.
   C. shares some of the same interests.
   D. all of the above

2. All of the following are ways to show you are listening to someone, except
   A. letting the speaker talk.
   B. giving advice.
   C. summarizing what the speaker says.
   D. asking questions.

3. You can avoid conflicts by
   A. explaining your opinions confidently.
   B. using good listening skills.
   C. avoiding putting down others.
   D. all of the above

4. To avoid angry feelings, you should
   A. discuss the problem with someone else.
   B. never take time to cool off.
   C. not take deep breaths.
   D. avoid exercise.

5. All of the following are causes of stress, except
   A. expecting too much of yourself.
   B. changing what you can and accepting what you cannot change.
   C. wanting to fit in.
   D. arguing with others.

6. One way you can tell that people are not listening is
   A. they interrupt.
   B. they face the speaker.
   C. they summarize what the speaker is saying.
   D. they make eye contact with the speaker.

Critical Thinking

How can peer pressure be helpful?
WRITING Suppose Keisha told everyone that she was not inviting Andrea to her Saturday night party. Now Andrea is very upset. Write an "I message" from Andrea to Keisha. Make sure Andrea's message does not attack Keisha.

Unit 3 > Your Health and Safety

Fresh fruits and vegetables are an important part of healthful eating. What other foods are important for your health?

Learning Objectives

- Describe a healthful diet.
- Identify the type of exercise that keeps you fit.
- Explain how alcohol, tobacco, and other drugs can be harmful.
- List ways to keep your body clean.
- Describe how to avoid dangerous situations.

Staying Healthy on Your Own

Words to Know

diet	everything that you eat or drink regularly
balanced diet	foods that provide your body with what it needs to stay healthy
serving	the amount of a food usually eaten at one time
prepared food	food that is treated in some way so it will last longer
ingredients	the parts of a prepared food
nutrition	the process of taking food into your body and using it for energy and growth
nutrients	the parts of food that your body needs to grow and stay healthy
calories	units that measure the amount of energy your body gets from food
vitamins	types of nutrients your body needs to stay healthy
aerobic exercise	an activity that makes your heart work harder
addiction	a physical dependence on a drug
germs	tiny life forms that can cause disease
risk	a chance that something harmful might happen

Read this paragraph about Mark. Sometimes he just grabs whatever is handy to eat and rushes off.

> Mark came home from soccer practice at 5:45. Shirley was picking him up in five minutes for their Community Youth Group meeting. He grabbed a cookie, some potato chips, and a can of soda. Then he went to watch for his ride.

Mark had a busy day. Because he was so busy, he had a snack instead of dinner. The snack he had did not give his body enough of the things it needs to work properly. He may feel tired later.

7-1 Choosing Healthful Food

Think about the snacks that Mark chose when he was in a hurry. He might have chosen a cup of yogurt, a handful of wheat crackers, and some orange juice. Instead he chose a cookie, potato chips, and soda.

Your **diet** is everything that you eat and drink regularly. A **balanced diet** provides all the foods

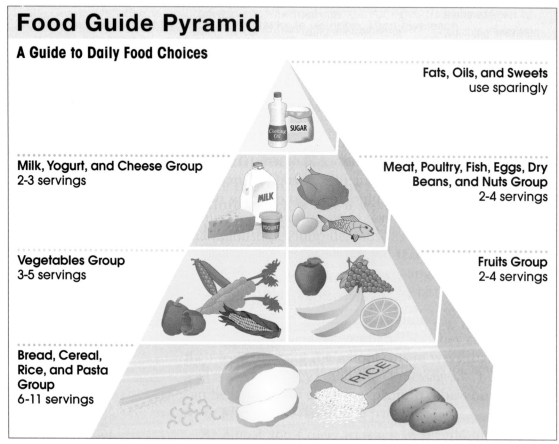

Food Guide Pyramid
A Guide to Daily Food Choices

Fats, Oils, and Sweets
use sparingly

Milk, Yogurt, and Cheese Group
2-3 servings

Meat, Poultry, Fish, Eggs, Dry Beans, and Nuts Group
2-4 servings

Vegetables Group
3-5 servings

Fruits Group
2-4 servings

Bread, Cereal, Rice, and Pasta Group
6-11 servings

Use this Food Guide Pyramid to help you choose a balanced diet.

that your body needs to stay healthy. Everyone needs a balanced diet.

Look at the Food Guide Pyramid on page 88. It divides foods into food groups. It explains how many servings you should eat from each food group every day to have a balanced diet. A **serving** is the amount of a food usually eaten at one time. Notice that you should eat more servings of the foods at the bottom of the pyramid each day and fewer servings of the foods at the top.

Mark's cookie, potato chips, and soda all fit in the Fats, Oils, and Sweets Group. Yogurt would have been a better choice for Mark. It fits into the Milk, Yogurt, and Cheese Group. Crackers would fit into the Bread, Cereal, Rice, and Pasta Group. Orange juice would fit into the Vegetables and Fruits Group. Those choices would have helped Mark better balance his diet for that day.

▶ **Everyday Tip**
Try to plan your meals ahead of meal time each day. When you are hungry, you do not always make healthful choices.

Practice

Write the name of the food group that each of these foods belongs to: carrots, rice, chicken, cornflakes, grapes, and frozen yogurt. Name three food groups found in a turkey sandwich with lettuce, tomato, and mayonnaise on whole wheat bread.

7-2 ▸ Becoming a Careful Food Shopper

When you shop, you can choose fresh or prepared foods. Fresh fruits and vegetables are usually the most healthful. These foods stay fresh only for a few days.

A **prepared food** is treated in some way so it will last longer. Prepared foods may be dried, smoked, or cooked, or they may have chemicals added to them.

Prepared foods have package labels. The package label lists what is in the food, or the **ingredients.** The ingredients are listed in order of the amounts present.

INGREDIENTS: Water, Lentils, Celery, Spinach, Tomato Paste, Dehydrated Onions, Salt, Olive Oil, Spices.

READY TO SERVE

0 52101 12101 7

This label is from a package of lentil soup. It lists the ingredients in the soup.

If the items listed on a package of trail mix are raisins, bananas, coconut, almonds, and apricots, that means the trail mix contains more raisins than anything else and more bananas than coconut.

Most prepared foods are mixtures, so the ingredients are parts of the mixture. Ingredients added to foods include such things as sugar, salt, and spices. Some foods also might have chemicals added that will make the food stay fresh longer.

Practice

Read the soup label shown above. List the three ingredients that make up the largest amounts in the soup.

7-3 ▶ Reading Nutrition Facts Labels

Nutrition is the process of taking food into your body and using it for energy and growth. A Nutrition Facts label lists some **nutrients** in the food. Nutrients are the parts of food that your body needs to grow and stay healthy. Some nutrients you might find on a food label are listed on the next page.

Nutrient	Purpose
fats (solid fats or oils)	needed in small amounts for growth and repair of body cells
carbohydrates (sugars and starches)	give your body energy
protein	needed for growth and repair of body cells
calcium	keeps bones and teeth strong
iron	keeps your red blood cells working
sodium	controls water balance in your body
vitamin A	needed for good vision
vitamin C	keeps gums, teeth, and bones healthy
water	keeps your whole body working properly

Look at the Nutrition Facts label on page 92. It tells you the amount of each serving, or serving size. It also tells you how many servings are in the package. Here are some of the things found on the label.

- *Calories* tells how many calories are in each serving. **Calories** are units that measure the amount of energy your body gets from food.

- *Calories from Fat* tells how many calories in a serving are from fat. A healthful diet is low in fat.

- *Total Fat* tells how many grams of fat are in a serving. One gram of fat is about 9 calories. If the label says the Total Fat is 4g, that means you get 9×4, or 36 calories per serving from fat. For a balanced diet, you need only a little fat. The lower the number of grams of fat, the more healthful the diet.

Nutrition Facts

Serving Size	1 cup (239g)
Servings Per Container	2

Amount Per Serving

Calories 90	Calories from Fat 20

	% Daily Value*
Total Fat 2g	3%
Saturated Fat 1g	3%
Polyunsaturated 0g	
Monounsaturated 1g	
Cholesterol 20mg	7%
Sodium 870mg	36%
Total Carbohydrate 13mg	4%
Dietary Fiber 2g	8%
Sugars 0g	
Protein 6g	

Vitamin A 30%	Vitamin C 0%
Calcium 2%	Iron 4%

*Percent Daily Values are based on a 2,000 calorie per day diet.

Mom's Hon
Soup

the best home-co

Gourmet Chi
with Wild R

Made with 100% Ch

This is a Nutrition Fact label. It is part of the food wrapper.

Practice

Answer these questions about the Nutrition Facts label above. Use a separate sheet of paper.

1. What is the suggested serving size?

2. How many calories are in one serving of soup?

3. How many calories are from fat in one serving?

7-4 ▸ Preparing Fresh Foods

The way you prepare food can change how healthful it is for you. Frying takes away some **vitamins** and adds fat. Vitamins are types of nutrients your body needs to stay healthy. If you boil vegetables in a pan full of water, you may destroy some vitamins, or they may come out of the vegetables and into the water. The most healthful way to cook any vegetable is to steam it.

To steam vegetables, add about half an inch of water to a pan. Bring the water to a boil. Then add the vegetables. Cover the pan and cook for a few minutes. You can buy a special basket called a steamer that will keep food out of the water while it cooks.

Practice

Work with a partner. Replace each snack listed below with one that would be more healthful. Then replace each activity with one that would make you more fit. Write your ideas on a separate sheet of paper.

Snacks: potato chips, candy bar, cookies, and soda

Activities: reading a magazine, watching TV, playing computer games

7-5 Exercising to Stay Fit

Exercise is important for staying healthy. You have more energy when you get regular exercise. Energy lets you think clearly and act quickly.

Exercise also helps people control their weight. People who take in more calories than they burn will gain weight. Exercise burns calories, so exercising can prevent weight gain or help a person lose weight.

▶ **Everyday Tip**
For your aerobic workouts, choose activities that you enjoy doing. That way you will not get bored.

The best kind of exercise to make you fit is **aerobic exercise.** Aerobic activity makes your heart work harder. Aerobic exercise helps strengthen your heart and blood system. For aerobic exercise to benefit you, you should do it for at least 20 minutes at a time at least three times a week. Running, bicycling, jumping rope, and dancing are good aerobic activities.

You can turn a daily activity into an aerobic exercise. For example, when you need to go somewhere, walk or ride a bike instead of riding in a car. If you walk a dog, walk fast, run, or jog part of the way.

Physical activities such as basketball are great ways to stay in shape and have fun.

Practice

On a separate sheet of paper, list three aerobic activities that you enjoy. Describe how you could combine them to make an exercise program.

7-6 Avoiding Alcohol, Tobacco, and Other Drugs

Now that you know how to choose healthful foods to put into your body, you also need to know what to keep out of your body. Alcohol, tobacco, and other drugs can harm your body. It is important to avoid them.

Certain drugs can help treat or cure illnesses if the drugs are used correctly. However, all drugs can be dangerous if they are used incorrectly. You should always follow the directions that come with the medicine. Never take someone else's medicine. A drug that helps one person could harm someone else.

Every drug changes the way your brain and body work. Always follow the directions on the label of a drug you buy at a store or one that is given to you by a doctor.

You should never take illegal drugs. Drugs can harm your body's organs very quickly. You may become very ill. Drugs also damage the body in ways that will not show up until later in life.

Driving a car after drinking or using other drugs is especially dangerous. You could have a serious accident. You could hurt yourself or someone else.

Using illegal drugs or misusing drugs you have bought at a store can become a habit. After a while, that habit can become an **addiction.** Addiction is a physical dependence on alcohol, tobacco, or another drug. Drug abuse can lead to crime, serious illness, and even death.

One harmful habit that leads to addiction is smoking. Smoking can cause heart disease, lung cancer, and a lung disease called emphysema. All of these conditions cause a slow death. Nonsmokers can get the same conditions by breathing secondhand smoke that is in the air.

Some people use smokeless tobacco. Two kinds of smokeless tobacco are chewing tobacco and snuff. People can get cancer of the mouth from smokeless tobacco.

Saying "No"

You know that using drugs can lead to addiction. Think about why people begin using drugs. Many young people try cigarettes, alcohol, or other drugs because other people tell them they should. Some people might pressure you and make you feel that you are not part of their group if you do not try what they suggest.

Using Technology

You can find answers to health questions on the Internet. For example, the American Lung Association Web site (www.lungusa.org) tells about the damage smoking does to the lungs.

Learning to resist peer pressure helps you carry out your decision not to use drugs. Making your own decision ahead of time will make resisting peer pressure easier. If people are your friends, they will want you to make your own decisions. They will also respect your decisions.

Some people try different drugs because they think it will make them feel good. They may think smoking, drinking, or using other drugs will make them look or feel more grown up. Or they may use drugs to try to escape from problems. But using drugs usually makes problems worse. Drug use also causes new problems.

It is important to learn to say "No" each time you are offered cigarettes, alcohol, or other drugs. It does not have to be hard to refuse drugs. It just takes confidence.

When someone offers you a drug, it may help to remember a few facts. Alcohol kills more teens every year than any other drug. Use of illegal drugs can kill the user at any time.

Practicing saying "No" can be helpful. Say it over and over in your mind. Practice with a friend or family member. Here are some other ways to say "No."

> No, I don't drink (or do drugs, or smoke).
>
> No, I'm allergic to smoke.
>
> NO WAY!
>
> No, I work hard to stay healthy.
>
> I promised my (father, friend, sister, self) I would stay away from drugs.

Did You Know

Star athletes warn young people about using drugs. At one time, most baseball stars chewed tobacco on the ballfield. Many of these stars now tell young people, "Don't start using tobacco or any other drug."

Practice

Write a warning about the problems of alcohol. Write your warning on a separate sheet of paper.

Keeping Your Body Clean

Good health means taking care of your body. One way to take care of your body is to keep it clean. Being clean helps you look and feel your best. It also helps prevent disease. Some **germs** carry disease. Germs are tiny life forms that are in the air.

Your hands may look clean but they still carry germs. The main way that germs get into your body is from your hands. When you put your hands near your mouth, nose, or eyes, germs that you cannot see can get into your body. For example, you can get a cold by shaking hands with someone who has a cold and then rubbing your eyes or nose.

Washing your hands with soap and water gets rid of most germs. Washing your hair keeps your hair and scalp clean. Baths or showers also wash away most germs. When germs and sweat combine, they cause odor. Deodorant helps to stop that body odor.

▶ **Everyday Tip**
Washing your hands is considered the most important way to prevent the spread of infection.

Extra oil may cause skin or scalp problems, such as acne or dandruff. You can choose a soap, shampoo, and deodorant to help handle these problems.

Your teeth and gums also need daily cleaning. Brushing after meals and at bedtime will help keep your teeth clean. Brushing is important to remove germs that cause tooth decay. Brushing will also help prevent bad breath.

Dental floss reaches places between teeth and gums that a toothbrush cannot reach. Tooth decay often starts between teeth near the gums. Keeping teeth clean is the best way to keep teeth and gums healthy.

Practice

On a separate sheet of paper, describe how each of these items can help you keep your body clean: soap, shampoo, deodorant, toothpaste, and dental floss.

Even when you take good care of your body, you need to protect yourself from other risks to your health. A **risk** is a chance that something harmful might happen. Avoid risks by being aware of what is around you. Ask yourself whether you are in a situation that could become dangerous. If your answer is "Yes," remove yourself from that situation.

Remember
Trust your own instincts about what is right and what is wrong. Do not let friends pressure you into an unsafe situation.

Know how to avoid danger and how to get away from a dangerous situation. Stay away from dark or deserted places. If you see someone you think might be dangerous, act on your feelings and avoid the person. Remember to trust your judgment.

If you think someone is following you, do not go to your home. Go to a police station or firehouse, a nearby business, or another public place. If someone starts following you, drive to a public place where there are many people. Always keep your car doors locked.

Always protect yourself from people who could hurt you. Never ride with a driver who has been drinking or taking drugs. Never get into a car with a stranger or let a stranger into your home. If someone at your door will not leave, call the police.

Avoid giving any personal information to strangers over the Internet or on the phone. Do not let a caller know you are alone. If you are going away overnight, ask your neighbors or friends to watch your home. Have them take in your mail and pick up your newspaper.

By using these hints, you can help keep yourself safe and reduce the risks of becoming a victim of crime.

Practice

Write a paragraph describing how you can protect yourself when you are in an unfamiliar place.

YOU DECIDE
How to Keep Safe

Read the story below. Then follow the steps to help Jake make a wise decision.

It was late one evening and Jake was home alone. He heard a loud knock at his door.

"Please let me use the phone," a woman's voice called through the door. "My car broke down." She sounded scared.

Jake had a problem. He did not want to refuse help to someone in need. But he knew he should never open his door to a stranger. He had to think carefully. How could he help the woman and protect himself from danger?

On a separate sheet of paper, follow the steps below to help Jake make a wise decision.

STEP 1   Identify the decision Jake must make.

STEP 2   List Jake's choices.

STEP 3   Cross out any choices that are harmful or might be against Jake's beliefs.

STEP 4   Think about the possible results of the remaining choices.

STEP 5   Select the best choice.

STEP 6   Explain how Jake would carry out his choice.

STEP 7   Describe the possible results of Jake's choice.

Make a Difference

What advice would you give Jake about opening the door and helping the woman?

Chapter

7 Review

Summary

For good health, eat a balanced diet. The Food Guide Pyramid and the Nutrition Facts labels on food packages can help you make healthful choices.
Aerobic exercise is helpful for staying fit. It makes the heart work harder so that more blood and oxygen reach all parts of the body.
To stay healthy, avoid using alcohol, tobacco, and other drugs. Drugs can become an addiction, which can ruin or end your life.
Keeping your body clean can help remove germs that cause disease. Being clean also helps you look good and feel good.
Taking care of your health includes staying away from danger. It is important to know how to avoid dangerous situations.

Vocabulary Review

balanced diet

serving

prepared food

ingredients

nutrition

calories

vitamins

aerobic exercise

addiction

germs

Write the term from the list that matches each definition below. Use a separate sheet of paper.

1. the amount of food usually eaten at one time

2. a physical dependence on a drug

3. tiny life forms that can cause disease

4. food that is treated so it will last longer

5. units that measure the amount of energy your body gets from food

6. foods that provide what you need to stay healthy

7. types of nutrients your body needs to stay healthy

8. the process of taking food into your body and using it for energy and growth

9. an activity that makes your heart work harder

10. the parts of a prepared food

Chapter Quiz

Write your answers in complete sentences.

1. How would you describe a balanced diet?
2. What is one difference between fresh foods and prepared foods?
3. What is one of the best types of exercises for staying fit?
4. What are two reasons to exercise?
5. Why is it important to keep clean?
6. What are three ways to avoid dangerous situations?
7. **CRITICAL THINKING** How can alcohol, tobacco, and other drugs cause harm?

Writing Activity

List all the foods you eat during a day. Compare what you ate to the Food Guide Pyramid on page 88. Then answer these questions in a paragraph.

1. Did I make sensible choices each time I picked something to eat? Why or why not?
2. What could I have chosen that would have been healthier?

Group Activity

In most states, the use of alcohol by persons under the age of 21 is against the law. What do you think of this law? Discuss your opinion in a small group. Then use the idea to write a scene to perform for the class.

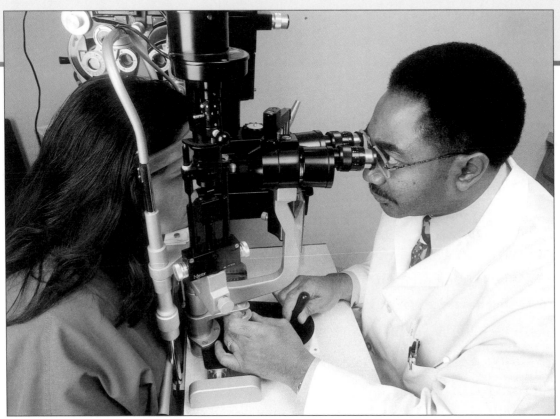

Getting regular checkups from your doctors can help prevent health problems later. Why do you think this is so?

Learning Objectives

- Identify what doctors and specialists do.
- Describe how to choose a doctor.
- Explain the advantages of checkups.
- Describe what happens during a checkup.
- Describe what to do before taking any medicine.
- Explain why health insurance is important.

Chapter 8 Getting Help With Your Health

Words to Know

specialists	doctors who treat only certain diseases or disorders
cavity	a hole in a tooth caused by decay
medical license	a document that gives a person the right to provide health care
symptom	a sign of illness or disorder
patient	a person under the care of a doctor
blood pressure	the push of the blood as it moves through your body
treat	to work to cure or relieve a disease or disorder
prescription	an order for medicine that a doctor provides
pharmacist	a person who prepares and gives out medicines that a doctor orders for you
over-the-counter medicines	medicines people can buy without a doctor's order; nonprescription drugs
ambulance	a special van driven by someone trained to help sick or hurt people and transport them to a hospital
emergency	a situation that needs to be taken care of quickly
health insurance	a plan that helps you pay for health care

Sometimes you might feel that something is not quite right with a part of your body. Perhaps, like Arlene in the story at the top of the next page, you have a problem with your teeth.

Arlene and Meghan were walking home. "Let's get some frozen yogurt," said Meghan.

Arlene shook her head. "No, I don't want any," she said. "It makes my teeth hurt."

"What does your dentist say?" asked Meghan.

"I don't know," Arlene answered. "I haven't been to the dentist in a long time."

"You should go. Maybe you have a cavity or something," said Meghan.

8-1 ▸ Learning About Doctors

Doctors are people trained and licensed to treat diseases and disorders. There are many kinds of doctors. Some are called general practitioners or family doctors. They can take care of most of your basic health needs. Doctors who treat only certain illnesses are called **specialists.** For example, an orthopedist is a doctor who treats the bones, joints, and muscles.

A dentist cares for the health of teeth and gums. Think about Arlene. Meghan thought Arlene might have a **cavity.** A cavity is a hole in a tooth caused by decay. If you have a cavity, you need to see a dentist.

Choosing a Doctor

To find a family doctor, ask family members and friends who their doctor is. Another way to find a doctor is to call a local hospital or medical society. Someone there can give you names of doctors near you. If you need a specialist, your doctor will recommend someone.

When choosing a new doctor, find out whether he or she has a **medical license.** A medical license is a document that gives a person the right to provide health care. Never go to a doctor who does not have a medical license.

Think About It

What do you think are the most important qualities of a good doctor?

Your doctor and his or her office staff should be friendly and helpful. It is important to get complete answers to your questions. It should also be easy to make an appointment with the doctor. An appointment is a set time to meet someone or do something. If you are sick, you want an appointment as soon as possible.

Finally, when choosing a doctor, think about how that doctor wants to be paid. Some doctors want to be paid right away. Others will send you a bill or send a bill to your medical insurer.

Practice

Suppose you need a new family doctor. Write a list of at least four questions to ask when you first call the new doctor's office.

8-2 Learning About Checkups

Most people go to a doctor when they are sick or hurt. However, people should also go to the doctor when they are well. Regular physical examinations, or checkups, help people stay healthy. Checkups can catch illness early. Many times, doctors find illness before a person sees or feels a **symptom.** A symptom is a sign of illness or disorder. For example, a sore throat is a symptom of a cold, the flu, or strep throat.

Finding an illness early can mean it will take less time to get well, or cured. Some diseases can be cured only if they are found before the **patient,** or person under the care of the doctor, has any symptoms. For example, many kinds of cancer can be cured if they are found early.

Getting a Checkup
When you go for a checkup, the doctor may ask you questions. You might be asked whether you are eating right or whether you get enough exercise and rest. The

▶ **Everyday Tip**
A symptom is a sign of an illness. It is not the illness itself. Remember to carefully explain all of your symptoms to your doctor during a visit.

doctor will ask whether you have any symptoms or whether there is anything you want to ask or discuss.

The doctor will examine your eyes, ears, throat, heart, lungs, and reflexes. The doctor may also check to see whether the other parts of your body look and feel okay.

During a checkup, your doctor also checks your **blood pressure.** Blood pressure is the push of the blood as it moves through your body. The doctor uses a machine to check your blood pressure. A blood pressure machine has a band that wraps around your arm. The band is attached to a plastic tube and ball.

If your pressure is too high, it can be harmful to your body. People may not know that they have high blood pressure. The only way to tell whether blood pressure is normal is to check it. Doctors can **treat,** or work to cure or relieve, high blood pressure before the patient has any problems.

During a checkup the doctor may take a small amount of your blood. You may also be asked to give a sample of your urine. The office sends the blood and urine to a lab for tests that can tell a lot about your health.

At the end of your checkup, the doctor will talk to you about it. This is a good time to ask questions about the checkup or your health. Usually, you need to call the office later to get your lab test results. If all goes well, you do not have to return to the office for another year.

If you have any symptoms of an illness, the doctor may order more tests. Suppose the tests show you have an illness. The doctor will explain to you what kind of treatment is available to treat that illness.

Practice

On a separate sheet of paper, list what happens when a person goes to the doctor for a checkup. Trade lists with a partner to see whether you forgot anything.

If you are sick or hurt, your doctor may write a **prescription**, which is an order for medicine. It is written on a special sheet of paper. You take the prescription to a drugstore. At the drugstore a **pharmacist** prepares and gives out medicine that the doctor ordered for you. Medicines that a doctor orders are called prescription medicines.

Medicines come with directions for taking them. The directions explain how much medicine to take and when to take it. They will be on the bottle or on a piece of paper that comes with the medicine.

Medicine directions may say "Take with food." That means you should take the medicine when you eat. Always follow the directions from the doctor or on the medicine package. Otherwise, the medicine will not work the way it should and you may be harmed.

People can buy some types of medicines without a doctor's order. These medicines include aspirin and cough medicine. They are called **over-the-counter medicines**, or nonprescription drugs. Use these medicines just as carefully as prescription medicines.

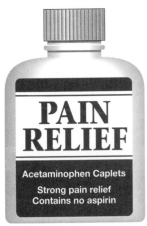

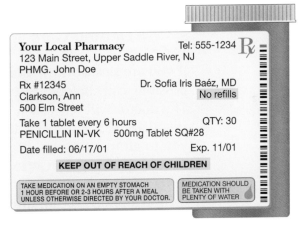

The bottle on the left is an over-the-counter medicine. The label on the right is for a prescription medicine.

Read everything on any medicine package. Notice whether it says "Exp." followed by a date. "Exp." is short for the word *expires*. After a medicine has expired, it should not be used. If the seal is broken or is not there when you buy the medicine, do not take it.

Both prescription medicines and over-the-counter medicines may have WARNING labels. They explain important facts you need to know. Be sure to read and follow the warnings. It is also important that you never take two different medicines at the same time unless your doctor tells you to. If you have questions about a medicine, call your doctor or pharmacist. They can answer your questions.

Practice

The directions below came from a medicine package. Use a separate sheet of paper to write each one again in your own words. Write a check mark next to each one that you think is a warning.

Keep out of reach of children.

May cause drowsiness.

Keep refrigerated.

8-4 ▸ Getting Care When Sick or Hurt

If you are sick or hurt, you should call a doctor. If possible, call the doctor that you see for your checkups. The doctor will tell you what to do over the telephone. If you are very sick or badly hurt, the doctor may tell you to go to a hospital. If you cannot reach your doctor, do not wait. Go to a hospital. If you are seriously hurt and cannot get to a hospital on your own, telephone for an **ambulance**. An ambulance is a special van driven by someone trained to help sick or hurt people. An ambulance can take you to a hospital.

Hospitals are always open. Hospitals have doctors, nurses, and equipment to handle an **emergency.** An emergency is a situation that needs to be taken care of quickly. Emergency rooms in hospitals handle emergencies.

Be prepared when you call or go to a hospital emergency room. Give as much information as you can. You will need to give a doctor or nurse your name, birthdate, insurance carrier, and reason for coming to the hospital. You will also need to explain your symptoms and any medicines you might be taking. You will be asked many questions. You need to work with the doctors and nurses so that they know how to help you.

Remember
Be honest and respectful when you talk to your doctor and dentist. These people are asking questions so they can help you stay healthy.

Understanding Health Insurance

Suppose your hand has been badly cut by broken glass. You go to the emergency room at the hospital. A doctor says you need stitches to close the cut, and the cost will be $500. Like many people, you may not be prepared to pay $500 on your own. If you have **health insurance,** it will probably pay for all or most of the cost. Health insurance is a plan that helps you pay for health care. Having insurance is called "being covered."

Health Choice USA		
NAME	COPAYS: OFFICE	10.00
Michaels, Bradley	OT/PT/SPEECH	10.00
MEMBER NUMBER	ER/URG CARE CENTER	25/15
734 153469524	EYE/EAR	15.00
BIRTH DATE EFFECTIVE CD	INPATIENT	00%
08-26-70 01-01-01 01	MENTAL HEALTH	20.00
PRIMARY CARE PHYSICIAN	ALLERGY	20%
Janis E. Withrop, M.D.	RX B	14.00
	G	8.00
Fully Insured SEE REVERSE	Health Choice, Inc.	

Your health insurance company may send you an insurance card as proof of membership. Take this card with you when you go to the doctor or dentist.

When you work full time, you may have insurance through your employer. Your employer pays a set amount to an insurance company for you and other workers each month. This is called group insurance. You and your employer share the cost of your health insurance. If you do not have group insurance, you need an individual policy. Then *you* would pay the set amount of money each month to the insurance company.

Shopping for Health Insurance

Health insurance plans can differ. You may be able to choose between traditional healthcare and a Health Maintenance Organization (HMO). In traditional healthcare you are able to choose your doctor. Under an HMO plan, you choose doctors from a list provided by your HMO. Shop around for a plan that works best for you. Figure out the total cost of each insurance plan for a year. You might also have to pay something for each doctor's visit and your prescriptions.

If you need to stay in a hospital, find out whether you have to pay part of the cost. The insurance company will probably pay most of it. Ask whether you can choose your own doctor. Some insurance groups have lists of doctors. Those insurance companies will pay only when you see doctors on their list.

If you buy an individual insurance policy, you may have an insurance agent. Make sure your agent is helpful. You are paying for a service with your policy.

When you are insured, you get an insurance card to carry with you at all times. Doctors and hospitals will ask to see this card when you need health care. You might have a separate card to use for buying your prescriptions.

Did You Know ?

Most insurance companies cover children up to age 23 on a parent's policy as long as the son or daughter is enrolled in school.

Practice

Answer the following question on a separate sheet of paper. What are three things you should ask about when choosing a health insurance plan?

YOU DECIDE
How to Help in an Emergency

Read the situation below. Then follow the steps to help Jamal decide what to do.

Jamal just moved to a new town. One night, he fell down the stairs in his new house. His leg hurt a lot. He thought it might be broken. Jamal had no doctor. He did not know anyone in his new town. He tried to stand, but he fell again. Jamal was in pain.

What should Jamal do?

On a separate sheet of paper, follow the steps below to help Jamal make a wise decision.

STEP 1 Identify the decision Jamal must make.

STEP 2 List Jamal's choices.

STEP 3 Cross out any choices that are harmful or might be against Jamal's beliefs.

STEP 4 Think about the possible results of the remaining choices.

STEP 5 Select the best choice.

STEP 6 Explain how Jamal would carry out this choice.

STEP 7 Describe the possible results of Jamal's choice.

Make a Difference
What advice would you give Jamal about getting help for his leg?

Summary

Doctors take care of people's health needs. Specialists take care of patients with specific problems.
Physical examinations, or checkups, help people stay healthy. Through checkups, doctors may find diseases early and be able to treat them more effectively.
In a checkup, the doctor who examines the patient may run tests.
Only doctors can order prescription medicines to treat illnesses. People can buy over-the-counter medicines without prescriptions. Always follow directions for using any medicine.
Health insurance helps people pay their doctor and hospital bills. People can shop for the insurance plan that meets their needs.

Vocabulary Review

Write *true* or *false* after each statement. If the statement is false, change the underlined word or words to make it true. Use a separate sheet of paper.

1. A <u>specialist</u> is a person under the care of a doctor.

2. An <u>emergency</u> is a situation that needs to be taken care of quickly.

3. Medicine ordered by a doctor is a <u>cavity</u>.

4. The push of blood as it moves through the body is <u>blood pressure</u>.

5. <u>Health insurance</u> helps you pay for health care.

6. A <u>patient</u> is a person who prepares and gives out medicines that a doctor orders.

7. Nonprescription drugs are called <u>over-the-counter medicines</u>.

8. A hole in a tooth caused by decay is a <u>prescription</u>.

Chapter Quiz

Write your answers in complete sentences.

1. Name one kind of specialist. What part of the body does this specialist care for?

2. What are three ways to find a doctor?

3. What is a checkup? What is one advantage of having checkups?

4. What are prescription medicines? What are over-the-counter medicines?

5. What should you do before taking any medicine?

6. What does a pharmacist do?

7. **CRITICAL THINKING** How does health insurance help you?

Writing Activity

Deanna and Charlotte both became sick with food poisoning after eating in a restaurant. They went to the emergency room at a hospital. Deanna had health insurance. Charlotte did not have health insurance.

Finish the story by describing what happened to each friend. Use a separate sheet of paper.

Group Activity

Working with a partner, look under "Insurance" in the Yellow Pages. Make a list of at least six words and phrases used to advertise insurance. Copy the ads that you use. How do the ads help you decide which insurance to choose? Share your ads and ideas with the rest of the class.

Smoke detectors give off a warning sound when they sense smoke. Each room of a house or an apartment should have one. How can you check that a smoke detector is working?

Learning Objectives

- Identify ways to make your home a safer place.
- Identify ways to be safer outside the home.
- List things you can do that can help avoid accidents.
- Explain ways to prepare for emergencies.
- Describe how to find help in an emergency.

Chapter 9 ▶ Staying Safe

Words to Know

smoke detector	a device that gives off a warning sound when it senses smoke
fumes	gases given off by chemicals
prepared	ready
fire extinguisher	a hand-held device used to spray special chemicals on a fire to put it out

There are many ways to make a home safe. Read the story below about a search for an apartment.

Joe was preparing to move to an apartment. His three best friends would be his roommates.

Joe's telephone rang. It was Mike. "I found a great place! Tell Carlo and Shawn, and let's meet there at 6:00 tonight." Mike gave Joe the address.

At 6:00 P.M., the friends met at the apartment. As they looked around, they began to smile.

"This place is great! Let's rent it." said Carlo.

"I love it too, but I see one problem," Joe said. "There is no smoke detector."

"So what?" Shawn said. "We don't smoke."

"We'll be careful in the kitchen," said Carlo.

"Fires can start for lots of reasons," said Joe. "There really should be a smoke detector here."

Mike turned to Joe. "Why don't we just buy a smoke detector? We can install it ourselves."

Joe, Mike, Shawn, and Carlo are taking on new responsibilities. They are planning to live on their own. All four are learning to see risks around them for the first time. A risk is a chance that something harmful might happen. The friends saw that there was a risk of fire in their new home.

Mike and Joe decided to install a **smoke detector**, a device that gives off a warning sound when it senses smoke. They proved that they were being responsible. Mike and Joe recognized the danger of fire. However, Shawn and Carlo were not thinking in a responsible manner.

9-1 ▶ Making Your Home Safe

Most accidents happen in the home. Fire is just one kind of risk in an apartment or any home. Accidental poisoning, electrical shock, cuts, and falls are other risks that could happen in the home. However, there are steps you can take to avoid each of these risks.

Using Technology

Many ovens have computerized timers. Set the timer whenever you cook something. Then you will know exactly when to check food and keep it from overcooking.

1. **Fire Safety:** Be careful when cooking. Stay in the kitchen while you cook. Handle pots and pans carefully to avoid burning yourself. Grease splattered during cooking can spark a fire, so keep stoves clean. Always remember to turn off stoves, ovens, and heaters after use. Outdoor barbecues and indoor fireplaces should feel cool before you leave them unattended or go to sleep.

   Keep things that can burn away from space heaters and heating vents. Also be careful with matches. Do not throw away anything that is burning or very hot. Make sure that no one smokes in bed. Finally, be sure to install smoke detectors.

2. **Poison Control:** Poison is another danger around the home. Medicines can be poisons if they are misused. Soaps and other cleaning supplies can

be poisons if you swallow them or breathe in the **fumes.** Fumes are gases given off by chemicals. Chemicals used for painting can also be poisons.

Make sure all medicines, cleaning supplies, chemicals, and other possible poisons are out of the reach of children and pets.

Think About It

Why is it important to keep chemicals away from small children and pets?

3. **Electric Safety:** Old or poorly made electrical wiring can cause an electric shock or a fire. You can get shocked if an electric current flows through your body. Check all wiring in the home. Replace worn or broken wires. Check that all electrical plugs fit tightly. There should not be too many plugs connected to one socket. To unplug an electrical cord, pull on the plug, not on the wire. Keep electrical products such as radios and hair dryers away from water. Do not touch them with wet hands. If you do, you could get shocked.

4. **Preventing Falls:** Many areas of the home are risky spots for falls. For example, slippery floors and stairs are places where people might fall and get hurt. To prevent falls, keep objects off the floors and stairs. When you need to reach up high, stand on a stable ladder or step stool instead of a chair. Chairs can break or fall over. Wipe up water spills right away. Put away toys, sports equipment, and tools.

5. **Avoiding Cuts:** Broken glass, knives, and other sharp objects can cause cuts. To avoid cuts, clean up broken glass with a broom or vacuum. Fix broken objects, and use knives carefully. Keep all sharp objects away from children. Handle tools carefully. Follow all directions for the safe use of power tools.

Practice

On a separate sheet of paper, list four risks in the home. Tell how to avoid each risk.

Accidents, injuries, and illness can also occur outside the home. Whether you are working or playing outdoors, you need to reduce the risks.

1. **Weather Safety:** One rule of outdoor safety is to be aware of the weather. Tornadoes, thunderstorms, heatwaves, and snowstorms cannot be prevented. But you can protect yourself by being prepared.

   Avoid the outdoors during thunderstorms. Go indoors or get in a car if you see lightning. If you must be outside in very hot weather, cover your head and drink lots of water. In very cold weather, dress warmly and stay dry.

2. **Travel Safety:** You also need to stay safe when you walk, jog, skate, drive, or ride your bicycle. One rule for all these forms of travel is to obey traffic lights and rules.

   Walkers or joggers should always look both ways for traffic when crossing a street. Do not cross in the middle of a block. If you are jogging at night, wear reflectors on your clothing so drivers can see you.

   Bicycle riders and skaters should wear safety equipment, especially helmets. Remember to ride or skate with the traffic, not facing it. Have a bell or whistle to warn others on the road and look out for people on foot.

3. **Car Safety:** To be safe in a car, everyone must wear a seatbelt. Never drink and drive. Do not ride with a driver who has been drinking. Also, try to talk someone out of drinking and driving. You could be saving a life.

Always wear your seatbelt whenever you ride in a car.

YOU DECIDE
What to Do in an Emergency

Read the situation below. Then follow the steps to decide what to do about Mara.

You are baby-sitting a two-year-old child named Mara. The phone rings and you talk to the caller for only a minute. When you hang up, you see Mara playing with bottles under the kitchen sink. Some of the bottles are open. You realize Mara has something smeared around her mouth.

On a separate sheet of paper, follow the steps below to help you make a wise decision.

STEP 1   Identify the decision you must make.

STEP 2   List your choices.

STEP 3   Cross out any choices that are harmful or might be against your beliefs.

STEP 4   Think about the possible results of the remaining choices.

STEP 5   Select the best choice.

STEP 6   Explain how you would carry out this choice.

STEP 7   Describe the possible results of your choice.

Make a Difference
What could you have done differently to keep Mara safe?

Summary

You can prevent accidents. Take actions to prevent a fire, an accidental poisoning, an electric shock, and other accidents in the home. Outside the home, follow safety rules at work and play.

Be prepared for accidents. Have smoke detectors and fire extinguishers around the home in case of fire.

Plan and practice a way for everyone to get out of the house in an emergency.

Know how to turn off the water and what to do if you smell gas.

Know how to get help in an emergency. Keep emergency numbers near each phone. In a public place, ask for help from someone nearby. Give as much information as possible when asking for help.

Vocabulary Review

smoke detector

fumes

prepared

fire extinguisher

Complete each sentence with a term from the list. Use a separate sheet of paper.

1. When people are ready, they are ____ .

2. A hand-held device used to spray special chemicals on a fire to put it out is called a ____ .

3. Gases given off by chemicals are called ____ .

4. A device that gives off a warning sound when it senses smoke is a ____ .

Chapter Quiz

Write your answers in complete sentences.

1. What is a risk? Give one example of a risk.

2. What are two ways to try to prevent fire in the home?

3. What steps can you take to prevent an accidental electric shock?

4. What are three kinds of telephone numbers that should be near each telephone?

5. What two things should you have in case of a fire? What do these things do?

6. What two things should you do if a water pipe breaks?

7. **CRITICAL THINKING** Why is it important to plan a way for everyone to get out of the house and meet in an emergency?

Writing Activity

Your eight-year-old brother, Tim, broke his leg. He will be in a cast for six weeks. What changes could you make in your home to make it safer for Tim while he is in a cast? Write your ideas on a separate sheet of paper.

Group Activity

Working in small groups, role-play one of the following situations. There is a small fire on top of the stove in your kitchen. Or, your dog has swallowed a household cleaner. You can create another situation if you choose. Use props. Invite the class to add ideas to your skit.

Unit 3 **Review**

Read each sentence below. Then choose the letter that best completes each one.

1. To stay healthy, you should avoid
   A. vegetables.
   B. drugs.
   C. fruit.
   D. dairy products.

2. Doctors are able to
   A. order prescription medicines.
   B. treat diseases and disorders.
   C. find illnesses during a checkup.
   D. all of the above

3. A good way to get help quickly in an emergency is to
   A. call 911.
   B. call a distant relative.
   C. call the pizza place.
   D. none of the above

4. When you keep your body and teeth clean, you
   A. look and feel good.
   B. prevent disease.
   C. prevent tooth decay.
   D. all of the above

5. All of the following are common directions for taking medicines, except
   A. take with food.
   B. take the whole bottle at once.
   C. keep out of reach of children.
   D. medicine should be taken with plenty of water.

6. If there is a fire in your house, you should
   A. breathe in the smoke.
   B. try to walk through the fire.
   C. cover your nose and mouth with a wet towel.
   D. jump from an upstairs window.

Critical Thinking

How are alcohol, cigarettes, and other drugs harmful to your health? **WRITING** Write a few paragraphs about what exercise does for your body. Include some examples of the ways you like to get exercise.

Unit 4 ▷ Getting and Keeping a Job

Chapter 10
Looking for a Job

Chapter 11
Getting a Job

Chapter 12
Keeping a Job

Chapter 13
Making the Most of a Job

A school or community job board is one place where you can find out about available jobs. What kind of job would you like to have after you finish school?

Learning Objectives

- Name your skills, interests, and personal qualities that would help you in certain jobs.

- Name several needs that a job can meet.

- Decide which job needs are most important to you now.

- Describe ways to learn about a job.

- Name sources of information about jobs.

Chapter 10 · Looking for a Job

Words to Know

personal qualities	ways you relate to other people and to the world around you
skill	something you do well
interest	something you care about or like to do
income	the amount of money you earn
flexible	able to change
career	the type of work a person does throughout his or her life to earn a living
informational interview	a discussion with someone who has a job that interests you, to learn more about that job

Read this story about what Floyd is thinking. Maybe you have faced the same type of situation.

Floyd often watched the people who rode the city bus with him in the mornings. He was on his way to school, but he wondered what kinds of jobs they had. Floyd was graduating from high school in a month. He knew he had to start looking for a job—and soon.

He noticed that some people riding the bus wore uniforms, suits, or dresses. Others did not. Some people looked bored, while others looked happy to be going to work. Floyd wanted to be one of the happy people. "Maybe I'll be a security guard," he thought. "Or maybe I'll work for a bank."

Before Floyd can choose a job, he has to find out what kinds of work he can do. He also needs to consider the type of work he wants to do. He needs to know what jobs are out there. Floyd must also think about his reasons for getting a job. He has to decide whether he just wants to earn money or he also wants to learn skills that may lead to a better job.

Finding the right job takes time and planning. First, you need to take a close look at yourself. You also have to figure out your strengths, interests, and needs.

10-1 ▸ Identifying Your Strengths

Your strengths include the **personal qualities** and skills that can help you do a job. Personal qualities are the ways you relate to other people and to the world around you.

People have many different personal qualities. For example, some people are comfortable talking with just about anyone. Others are willing to listen and consider

An outgoing personality is an important quality for a person who works with the public.

different points of view. Some people are eager to help. Still others are more concerned about their own needs.

Some jobs require specific personal qualities. For example, someone in sales should be outgoing and full of energy. A child care worker needs to be calm and gentle and should love children. A security guard should be firm and careful. Being dependable is a good personal quality for any job.

Your strengths also include your **skills.** A skill is something you do well. For example, you might be good at solving math problems or fixing motors. Perhaps you know how to help people settle arguments. You might speak a foreign language or know how to type. You also have to think about your skills when choosing a job.

Practice

On a separate sheet of paper, list personal qualities from the chart below that describe you. Next, add words that describe your skills. Then write three jobs that might call for your personal qualities and skills.

Personal Qualities		
forceful	organized	friendly
calm	artistic	dependable
careful	outgoing	fair
full of energy	cheerful	independent
cooperative	helpful	creative
firm	thoughtful	patient

10-2 ▸ Identifying Your Interests

Just because you are good at something does not mean you like to do it. For example, you might be good at cleaning but hate to clean. It might really bore you.

Consider your interests when you look for a job.

If you know this, you may not want to apply for a job on a cleaning crew. You could do that job well, but you would probably not be happy doing it.

It is important to think about what you like to do. Consider your **interests** when thinking about jobs. An interest is something you care about or like to do. Some people are interested in working with computers. Others want to help clean up the environment. Still others are interested in exercising or in growing plants.

Practice

On a separate sheet of paper, list at least six of your interests. Then consider your skills. Work with a partner to think of jobs that might use both your interests and skills. Share your ideas with the class.

You must decide what you need from a job before choosing one. Nearly everyone works to earn money to pay for basic needs. Basic needs include housing, food, and clothing. You also might have other needs in a job.

Income is the amount of money you earn. You might be looking for a job that pays well. Maybe you want to buy a car or get an apartment. Your goal is to earn as much money as possible.

While you are in school, you might want a part-time job. Working in the evenings or on weekends might fit in with your classes and study routine. You might also think about looking for a part-time job that could become a full-time job after you graduate.

You might need a job with **flexible** hours. Flexible means "able to change." For example, if you have an important test in a week, you need to study. If you have flexible hours, you might be able to work fewer hours *before* your test and *more* the next week.

You also need a job you can get to easily. If you have a car, you need to think about how long you want to spend driving to and from work. If you do not have a car, you need to be able to take a bus or train. Remember to consider the cost of getting to a job.

Sometimes people take jobs just so they can learn skills for better jobs. For example, working in a day-care center might help someone get a job as a teacher's aide in an elementary school later on.

Jobs take place under many different working conditions. You may like working indoors better than working outdoors. You may prefer a physical job in which you use your strength. Or you might want a job in which you discuss ideas or solve problems.

Think About It

Which is more important to you, a higher income with poor working conditions or a lower income with good working conditions?

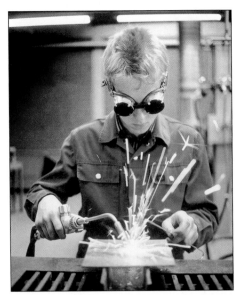 

Different jobs have different working conditions.

Working conditions are important to think about when deciding on a job. If you are happy with your working conditions, you will be happier with your job. For example, if you do not like being outdoors, you would not be happy working as a trail guide.

Jobs can also meet emotional needs. Some people work in hospitals because they feel good about helping others. Others work in auto repair shops because they like cars. Choose a job that fits your needs, skills, and interests.

Practice

What do you need from a job? On a separate sheet of paper, list at least three of your needs. Compare them to your list of jobs from the Practice on page 132.

10-4 ▶ Choosing a Job and a Career

Your job needs right now might vary greatly from your job needs in five or ten years. You need to think about what you want for your future. You need to plan for a

career. A career is the type of work a person does throughout his or her life to earn a living.

Very few jobs will meet all your needs perfectly. You often have to give up some things in order to get other things. For example, you might find a job that pays well and could lead to an even better job. However, that job might be 45 minutes away. You have to decide whether the pay and opportunities are worth the long trip. Remember, you will need to take that trip ten times each week.

Or maybe you are looking for a full-time job in a restaurant. The only job you can find is at a nearby restaurant, but it is only part time. You decide to take it. It is possible that the job could change. It could become a full-time job. By working part time now, you might get the job you really want later on.

Deciding which job to take can be difficult. It requires balancing the things you like about a job with the things you may not be happy about. You must also think about your job needs now and your career needs for the future. You might change your mind many times before you find the career you want.

Remember
Too many activities can cause stress. Be realistic about what you can do.

Practice

On a separate sheet of paper, make a list of six needs that a job can meet. Then put the needs in order of importance for you right now. Write your most important need at the top. Explain why you put the needs in that order.

10-5 ▸ Gathering Information About Jobs

You have identified your personal qualities, skills, and interests. You have thought about which job needs are most important to you. Now it is time to find out more about jobs that might suit you.

Your school guidance counselor might have information about types of jobs. Your library or the Internet may have these books, which describe thousands of jobs.

- *Occupational Outlook Handbook*
- *Dictionary of Occupational Titles*
- *Occupations Digest*

These books explain the kinds of training jobs require and how much they pay. They also explain which job fields are growing and need more workers.

One of the best ways to find out about a job is to talk with someone who has that job. This is called an **informational interview**. During an informational interview, you are not asking for a job. You are just asking for more information about the job and the company. Your school guidance counselor, family, or friends might know people who have jobs that interest you. They might help you set up meetings with these people. Then you could find out more about these jobs. You can see whether they still interest you.

Before your informational interview, make a list of questions to ask. Here are some examples.

- What kinds of things do you do on your job?
- What skills do you need to do this job?
- What special training did you have that helped you get this job?
- What do you like best about your job?
- What do you like least about it?

Do not ask the person how much money he or she makes. However, you can ask about the average pay for someone in that job or about starting salaries for entry-level jobs in that field.

To set up an interview, call and ask whether the person is willing to meet with you. Set a time to meet. Then arrive on time, looking your best. After the interview, write a thank-you note to the person or people you met. Remember, you might ask the same person to hire you some day!

An informational interview can help you figure out whether you are interested in and qualified for a certain job.

Finding Out What Is Available

Now you know more about jobs you think you would like and could do well. The next step is finding out what jobs are available. Be sure to tell friends and family members you are looking for a job. They might know of openings that would suit you.

Your school or local library may have a bulletin board of job openings in the area. You might also see "Help Wanted" signs in store windows. State agencies may have phone numbers you could call to learn about available jobs.

Your newspaper can also help you learn about the job openings in your community. Look for the "Want Ads" or "Employment Guide" sections of the paper. Jobs are usually grouped under headings such as "Secretarial/Clerical" or "Sales." The job openings under each heading are listed in alphabetical order.

"Want Ads" can also tell you what kind of jobs have the most openings. For example, you may find ten want ads under "Restaurants/Hotels" for cooks. However, you might find nearly 100 ads under "Computers." These jobs are for people who know how to use computers. If you are interested in computers, you might take some courses on word processing or programming. Then you would have a much wider choice of jobs.

"Want Ads" abbreviate some words to save space. Here are some examples.

Abbreviation	Meaning
f/t	full time (usually 40 hours a week)
p/t	part time (less than 40 hours a week)
Exp. req.	experience required
c/o	in care of (the address to write to)
Attn.	attention (the person to write to)
E.O.E.	Equal Opportunity Employer (This employer does not hire or reject people because of their age, race, sex, or disability.)

Practice

Look in a newspaper for the "Want Ads" section. Cut out two ads that seem interesting and that meet your needs and skills. Circle all the abbreviations and write what you think each one means. Use a separate sheet of paper.

YOU DECIDE
How to Choose the Right Job

Read about Dolores. Then follow the steps to help her make a job decision.

Dolores wants to share an apartment with a friend. She will need $750 a month for rent and other expenses. She loves people and wants to learn more about art. She has been offered the two full-time jobs listed below.

Job 1 Ticket-seller at a theater. She would work alone in the ticket booth. She would be paid $950 a month.

Job 2 Assistant to a newspaper cartoonist. Dolores would help the cartoonist and learn what he does. She would be paid $850 a month.

On a separate sheet of paper, follow the steps below to help Dolores decide which job to take.

STEP 1 Identify the decision Dolores must make.

STEP 2 List her choices.

STEP 3 Cross out choices that are harmful or against Dolores's beliefs.

STEP 4 Think about how each choice fits Dolores's personal qualities, skills, interests, and needs.

STEP 5 Select the best choice for her right now.

STEP 6 Explain why this is the best choice for her.

STEP 7 Describe how this job might affect Dolores, now and in the future.

Make a Difference
How would you explain to Dolores the process you went through to choose a job?

Summary

Before you look for a job, think about your personal qualities, skills, and interests. Try to choose a job that matches these things.
A job can fill a need for income, scheduling, location, training and education, working conditions, and personal satisfaction. You must decide which needs are most important to you.
People's job needs change over the years. They have to decide how well a job meets their needs at a particular time in their life. They also have to think about the future and their career goals.
To learn more about certain jobs, go to the library or go online. Several books describe different kinds of jobs. You can set up informational interviews to talk with people who have jobs that interest you.
Libraries and some state agencies have information about available jobs in the community. Newspaper Want Ads and Internet sites also list available jobs. They also show which job fields have more openings.

Vocabulary Review

income

interest

skill

personal qualities

informational interview

career

flexible

Write the term from the list that matches each definition below. Use a separate sheet of paper.

1. able to change

2. something you care about or like to do

3. work that people do throughout their lives to earn a living

4. something you do well

5. how you relate to other people

6. a discussion with someone who has a job that interests you, to learn more about that job

7. the amount of money you earn

Chapter Quiz

Write your answers in complete sentences.

1. Before you look for a job, what are three things you should consider about yourself?

2. What are four examples of personal qualities?

3. What are four examples of skills?

4. Does everyone have the same job needs? Why or why not?

5. Why should you find out how far away a job is from your home?

6. What can newspaper "Want Ads" tell you about jobs?

7. **CRITICAL THINKING** What are at least four questions you could ask during an informational interview?

Writing Activity

Find a job in the "Want Ads" that you think you would like. Write a paragraph to describe how that job fits your personal qualities, skills, and interests. Include some needs that the job might meet for you.

Group Activity

Parents often suggest that their teenagers apply for certain jobs. In a small group, discuss whether a parent should try to influence a teenager's choice of jobs. Should this decision be left completely up to the teenager? Why or why not? Write your ideas and explain your group's opinion to the class.

To get the job that you want, you need to show that you are the best person to hire. How might you convince an employer to hire you?

Learning Objectives

- Describe the kinds of information found on a résumé and in a cover letter.

- Explain how to fill out a job application.

- Explain how to prepare for a job interview.

- Give examples of common questions asked at interviews and ways to answer them.

- Explain how to decide between job offers.

- Give examples of job benefits.

Chapter **11** Getting a Job

Words to Know

résumé	a summary of your education and work experience
references	people who know you well and will tell employers that you are a good worker
cover letter	a letter to introduce you to an employer
job application	a form you fill out when applying for a job
Social Security number	a number assigned to each person by the government; a form of identification
interview	a meeting in which you answer another person's questions about yourself
job benefits	health insurance, vacation time, and other things you receive in addition to your salary

There are many skills that are important for getting a job. Read the story below, and see what happened to Tyler.

Tyler read the woman's name tag. It said she was Barbara Cole, store manager. "Just the person I should talk to," Tyler thought.

"Excuse me, Ms. Cole," Tyler said in a confident and friendly voice. "I hear you are hiring salespeople. I'd like to apply for that job."

Ms. Cole nodded and said, "Please leave your résumé. I'll read it this afternoon."

Tyler swallowed hard. He did not have a résumé, so he could not leave one. Tyler would not get the job without a résumé.

Getting a job is not easy. You have to prove you are the best person to hire. Knowing how to write a strong résumé and how to fill out a job application form will help. Preparing for the job interview is also important. This chapter will help you increase your chances of getting the job you want.

11-1 ▶ Writing a Résumé

A **résumé** is a summary of your education and work experience. It is best to limit this summary to one page. The purpose of a résumé is to convince an employer to call you for an interview. Your résumé should introduce your work experience to the employer.

Miriam Ashaad
222 Yearling Avenue
Durham, North Carolina 27701
(919) 555-4199

Objective: Assistant food manager in a supermarket or restaurant

Work Experience:

1/01–present   Chef's Assistant. Boyle's Restaurant. Ordered supplies; supervised kitchen staff.

7/00–1/01   Server. Judy, Judy, Judy Caterers. Supervised two servers.

3/00–6/00   Server. Let's Eat Catering Company. Served 1,000 people for a Feed-the-Homeless event.

Education: Graduated from Williams High School, June 2001
Durham Adult Education courses:
"Cooking for Families," July 2000
"Basic French Cooking," July 1999
"Kids Can Cook, Too!" July–August 1998

Skills: Can manage and serve meals for large groups
Good business and "people" skills

Look at Miriam's résumé on page 144. It will help you see how to write the information needed in a résumé.

1. Your full name, address, and phone number should go at the top of the page. Use large letters or bold type. Make it easy for the employer to know how to contact you. Then describe your objective or the kind of job you would like to have. However, many people choose to describe their job objective in a letter. The letter would go with the résumé.

Using Technology
There are Web sites that will give you information on how to write a résumé.

2. The most important section of your résumé is the list of your work experience. Start with the job you have or the last job you had. Write the date each job started and ended. Include the company name and your job title. If you do not have any experience in working for an employer, list your volunteer work. You can also list jobs such as baby-sitting, lawn mowing, or other things you have done to earn money. Include any information on the job that an employer would want to know. For example, Miriam was a server. However, she does not say that she served customers. The reader already knows that. Instead, Miriam says that she also supervised people. This is something an employer would want to know because it shows she is responsible.

3. A list of when and where you went to school and graduated should also be included on a résumé. Include any classes or courses you have taken that would help you on the job you want. This education section should come first if you are still in school or have just graduated. It can be last if you have been out of school for a long time.

4. Include a section on skills at the bottom of your résumé. Describe things you do well that will help you on this job. List any of your interests that relate to this job. Name any honors or awards you have won.

Résumé Do's and Don'ts

Always tell the truth in your résumé. If an employer finds out you lied on your résumé, you will not get the job.

▶ **Everyday Tip**
Keep your résumé up-to-date. Add or change information as you gain experience and skills.

Remember that your résumé introduces you. If it is messy or has spelling mistakes, you will look bad. Make sure your résumé is neat, complete, clear, and well organized. Then the employer will be more likely to call you for an interview.

Another rule to follow when preparing a résumé is to start each description with a strong verb. Avoid *I, me,* and *my.* For example, don't write "I took orders from customers." Instead, start with a strong verb, "Handled customer orders."

Add details and numbers to show that you did your job well. For example, do not just write, "Answered the phones." Instead, write "Answered phones and took messages for four attorneys."

There are also some things you should not include when preparing your résumé. Do not explain why you left a job. You can do that during your interview. You do not have to list your age, race, ethnic background, religion, or sex.

Practice

On a separate sheet of paper, rewrite each sentence below. Change it so it could be included in a résumé. The first one is done for you.

1. I cut the grass for my neighbors.
   Mowed 12 neighbors' lawns.

2. I took the customers' money for the jobs.

3. Sometimes I made lunch for the children.

4. The boss asked me to order supplies.

11-2 ➤ Using References

References are people who know you well and will tell employers that you are a good worker. You list references on a job application or in a letter to an employer. Choose people who can give an employer a good description of you and your work.

A reference might be a person you have worked with in the past. You might list a teacher who knows your work. Do not use family members. Give a list of your references to employers when they ask for it. Include each person's name, job title, address, and phone number.

Some forms you fill out for jobs will ask you to list references. Before you list any references, be sure to call these people yourself. Ask whether they are willing to speak to employers about you. Then your references will not be surprised when an employer calls them.

Practice

On a separate sheet of paper, list three people you might use as references. Call these people before you give out their names. Include phone numbers where an employer can contact them during the day. Save this list in case you need to give references to an employer.

11-3 ➤ Writing a Cover Letter

To make a good impression, send a **cover letter** along with your résumé. A cover letter helps introduce you to an employer. You might send the same résumé to different companies. However, you should write a different cover letter for each job. Your cover letter should describe why you want to work for that company. You might stress the skills and experiences that would help in that job. Read the cover letter on page 148 that Miriam wrote to Mitchell's Food Mart.

222 Yearling Avenue
Durham, North Carolina 27701

June 29, 2001

Manager, Mitchell's Food Mart
100 Main Street
Durham, North Carolina 27701

Dear Manager:

I would like to apply for the position of assistant food manager. I saw your ad in Sunday's <u>Durham Times</u>. I shop at Mitchell's often and would really like to work there.

My résumé is enclosed. As you will see, I just graduated from Williams High School. For the past three summers I have taken business courses. I love to work with others, and I want to begin working on my career.

I hope to pursue a career in food management. A position with your company would fit perfectly with my career plans. Please call me at 919-555-4199 if you have any questions or would like further information. I hope to hear from you soon.

Sincerely,

Miriam Ashaad

Miriam Ashaad

Practice

Choose a company you would like to work for. Write a cover letter for a job opening in that company.

11-4 ▶ Filling Out a Job Application

When you apply for a job, you might be asked to fill out a form called a **job application.** Job applications often ask for the same information that is on a résumé.

However, some companies want to have the information on their forms instead of a résumé.

The form will ask for your **Social Security number.** This is a number assigned to each person by the government. Each U.S. citizen has a Social Security number. It is a form of identification employers use.

In addition to asking for the same information that is on a résumé, a job application may also ask these questions:

- How long have you lived at your current address?

- Are you a citizen of the United States?

- How did you learn about this job?

- Have you ever been convicted of a felony?

- Whom should we contact in case of emergency?

- When could you start work?

Read the whole application before filling it out. Ask for two copies of the application. If you make a mistake, start over. Check your spelling. Be sure the dates are correct.

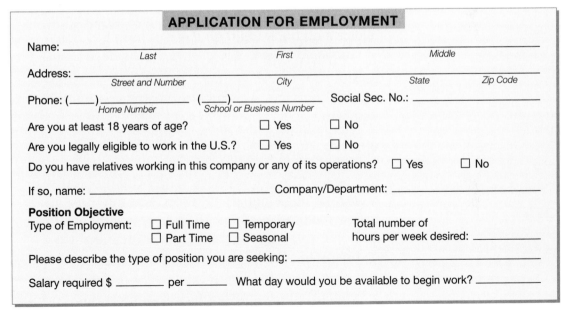

This is one section of a job application.

Do not write in the sections marked "For Employer Only." Fill in the other sections. Some questions may not apply to you. Just leave these sections blank or write "N/A," which means "Not Applicable."

Job Screening

Some companies ask you to take a test as part of your job application. For example, a company might ask you to take a typing or computer test. If the job is putting small parts together, you might have to show that you can do it. A few companies may ask you to complete a drug screening test. You can always refuse to take these tests. However, if you refuse, you may not get the job.

Practice

Choose five questions from the list on page 149. Write answers for them on a separate sheet of paper.

11-5 ▸ Preparing for Job Interviews

The next step in getting a job is doing well during the job **interview**. During a job interview, someone from the company will ask you questions about yourself. Your answers will help the employer decide whether to hire you. You might meet with the store manager for the interview. At a large company, you might talk with someone in the human resources or personnel department. These departments interview and hire people for large companies.

Be prepared for an interview when you drop off your résumé or fill out an application. You might be asked to talk to someone then. Usually, you will have to go home and wait for a call from someone at the company to schedule an interview.

Think About It

Why is it important to be dressed neatly when you drop off a résumé or fill out a job application?

If someone calls to arrange an interview, set it up as soon as possible. The day of the interview, be sure to arrive on time. The day before, travel to the store or company office. Then you will know how long it will take to get there. Make sure you look your best. Always dress neatly for the interview.

Preparing for an Interview

Prepare before you go to an interview. Find out as much as you can about the company. Talk to anyone you know who works there. Try to learn as much as possible about the job.

Think of questions you might be asked during the interview. Plan how you will answer each question. Be prepared to explain why you want to work there and why they should hire you. You could describe

Using Technology

Most large companies and some small ones have Web sites. You can usually learn about the company's history, business, and other information on their site.

Always dress neatly and appropriately for an interview.

what you like about the company or how working for the company could help you meet your career goals. Stress that you know you can do a good job and that you are also eager to learn new things.

You might be asked to point out your strengths and weaknesses. For your strengths, name some things that would help you do the job well. Working on a team or solving problems could help on a job where you might work closely with others. For your weaknesses, think of a positive way to describe a weakness. You might say that you do not know much about word processing. However, you are taking a course so you can learn. Avoid giving a weakness that will make you look unfit for the job.

Handling an Interview

You may feel nervous during your interview. The interviewer will expect that. Try to relax. Remember that this is not your only chance to get a job. You will have many more interviews. You will learn from each one. You will get better at answering questions and staying calm. Each interview is a learning experience.

During the interview, look the other person in the eye. Sit up straight to show you are sure of yourself. Speak clearly and avoid using slang.

You should also ask questions during the interview to find out whether the job is right for you. Good questions show that you are serious about wanting the job. One question you might ask the interviewer is to describe the type of person the company wants for this job. Then you can explain why you are the one to hire. If you cannot work certain hours, ask what days and hours you would have to work. You might find that you could not work the hours the job requires.

During the interview, the interviewer probably will not tell you whether you got the job. The company has to compare you with other people applying for the job.

They will decide who will get the job later. It sometimes takes several days or weeks to decide.

After the interview, always send a thank-you letter as soon as possible. Include a sentence or two about why you would be perfect for the job. If you have decided you do not want the job, politely explain why.

Practice

Work in groups of three to practice a job interview. One person will be the interviewer. The second person will be applying for a job. The third person will watch and listen. Together, write details about the company and the job. Write questions to ask. Then start the interview. Afterward, the third person will help the other two decide what went well and what needs improvement.

11-6 ▸ Choosing Between Jobs

You might not get the job you want. Very few people get every job they apply for. However, you might get job offers from different places. Then you will have to choose between them. You will have to decide which job best meets your needs.

Remember
It is important to choose a job that fits your needs, skills, and interests.

To do this, think about which job pays enough to cover all your expenses. Maybe one has better hours or a more flexible schedule. Also think about travel time and transportation costs.

You will want a job that is interesting and important to you. You might also look for a job that offers training or courses that will prepare you for a better job in the future.

Working conditions should also be considered. If you like to work with people, you may want to be part of a team. If you like to work outside, an office job might be the wrong choice for you. Finally, think about which one has the better job benefits.

Understanding Job Benefits

Job benefits may include health insurance, vacation time, and other things you receive in addition to your salary. Part-time employees often do not receive the same benefits as full-time workers.

Having health insurance is very important. Many companies pay part of the cost of health insurance. Then each employee pays his or her share. This can range from a small cost to a few hundred dollars a month. Before you accept a job, find out how much this cost will be. If you need health insurance and the job does not offer it, you might want to look for another job.

Vacation days and sick days may also be job benefits. A number of companies also pay for courses so their employees can learn new skills. Other companies offer excellent savings or retirement plans for employees. Learning about these benefits can help you decide whether to take a job.

Getting the Job

The process of getting a job can be complicated, but you can do it. Now you know how to write a résumé and a cover letter. You can fill out a job application. You have learned what to do before and during a job interview. You even know how to choose between two jobs. You are ready to search for a job!

Practice

Talk about vacation days and sick days with a family member or friend who is working full time. Find out whether most companies give the same number of vacation and sick days to employees. Write down what you learn.

Read the story below. Then follow the steps to help Alexis make a decision.

Alexis left her apartment at 10:20 A.M. for her job interview. The interview was at 11:00 A.M. with Mr. Blake. Alexis knew where the office building was located. It would take her 15 or 20 minutes to drive there. Then she could park and get to Mr. Blake's office in plenty of time.

BAM! Was it a flat tire? Alexis pulled over to the side of the road. Sure enough, her right back tire was flat. Alexis knew how to change a tire. She also knew that changing it would make her late for her interview. And it would make her dirty.

On a separate sheet of paper, follow the steps below to help Alexis decide what to do.

STEP 1 Identify the decision Alexis must make.

STEP 2 List her choices.

STEP 3 Cross out any choices that are harmful or might be against Alexis's beliefs.

STEP 4 Think about the possible results of each remaining choice.

STEP 5 Select the best choice for Alexis.

STEP 6 Tell how Alexis would carry out that choice.

STEP 7 Describe how this decision might affect Alexis's job interview.

Make a Difference
What advice would you give Alexis about getting to a job interview the next time?

11 Review

Summary

| To apply for a job, you may need to write a résumé. |
| Write a cover letter to send with every résumé. A cover letter introduces you and explains why you want the job. |
| A job application form asks for some of the same information that is in a résumé. Fill it out accurately, completely, and neatly. |
| During a job interview, a company employee will ask you questions. Prepare for a job interview by learning all you can about the job and the company. Plan your answers to questions that the interviewer might ask. |
| On the day of an interview, you should look your best and be on time. Try to relax and answer the interviewer's questions with confidence. |
| To choose between jobs, decide which one better meets your needs. |
| Job benefits can include health insurance, vacation days, and sick days. |

Vocabulary Review

Write *true* or *false.* If the statement is false, change the underlined word or words to make it true. Use a separate sheet of paper.

1. A summary of your education and work experience is a <u>cover letter</u>.

2. A meeting in which you answer another person's questions about yourself is an <u>interview</u>.

3. People who know you well and will tell employers that you are a good worker are called <u>references</u>.

4. A number assigned to each person by the government, or a form of identification, is called a <u>Social Security number</u>.

5. Health insurance and vacation time are kinds of <u>salary</u>.

Chapter Quiz

Write your answers in complete sentences.

1. What information should be included on a résumé?

2. Why should you write a cover letter?

3. Why is neatness important on a résumé, cover letter, and job application?

4. What should you do to prepare for a job interview?

5. What should you do during a job interview?

6. What are some examples of job benefits?

7. **CRITICAL THINKING** How would you answer if an interviewer asked you to name some of your strengths and weaknesses?

Writing Activity

Some parents arrange for their children to be hired by the company where the parents work. Do you think it should be against company rules to hire the children of employees? Why or why not? Write your ideas on a separate sheet of paper.

Group Activity

In a small group, brainstorm how to handle a job interview. Then create a script for a job interview. Finally, role-play the interview for the class.

On the first day of a new job, it is natural to feel a bit nervous. Just remember that you were chosen for the job. You can do it. What could you do to prepare for it?

Learning Objectives

- Explain ways to do well on the first day at work.
- Describe the kinds of information in an employee handbook.
- Describe actions that will help you keep your job.
- Identify ways problem solving can help you get along at work.
- Explain why it is important to learn new skills on a job.

Chapter 12 ▷ Keeping a Job

Words to Know

co-workers	people who work for the same company
employee handbook	a book that describes company rules and job benefits
fired	dismissed from a job
schedule	a list of times to do things
shift	a period of time for work
deadline	the latest time something can be done
layoff	a period of time when a company has no work for employees

The first day on any job can make new employees feel a little unsure of themselves. Read the story below, and see how Juanita felt on her first day.

"I'm very nervous," Juanita said to her cousin Carl. "It's my first day at my new job."

Juanita was getting ready for her new job at a radio station. She knew she had the skills. She also knew the job had many responsibilities.

"You'll do fine!" Carl said.

"But what if I forget something?" Juanita was getting more and more worried. "What if I forget that the red light means 'On the Air'?"

Carl tried to calm her. "Your supervisor doesn't expect you to remember everything on your first day. She just expects you to do your best."

Carl was right. Like Juanita, many people are nervous on their first day at a new job. Employers expect new people to be nervous. However, it is important to make a good impression. Employers are more concerned about what employees will do after their first day. They are more concerned with new employees getting along with their supervisors, other employees, and customers. Employees have to learn new skills and follow a schedule. They may have to work on a team. This chapter will help prepare you for your first day at work and for the days after that.

12-1 ▸ Planning for the First Day

On your first day at a new job, remember that you were chosen for this job. Your employer is confident that you can do it. That is why you were hired.

Your first day will go more smoothly if you follow these tips.

1. First, be on time and dress neatly and correctly for your job. If you are not sure what to wear, call the person who offered you the job. Ask what you should wear.

Remember
Be positive and confident.

2. Next, try to relax and be yourself. Stay calm. Remember that most problems will work themselves out after a while. No mistakes are permanent. Just do your best.

3. On your first day, you will probably meet many new people, including **co-workers.** Your co-workers are the people who work for the same company as you. You will slowly learn their names as you work with them. However, you should learn your supervisor's name right away. Write it down so you will not forget it. Find out how it is spelled in case you have to write him or her a note.

4. Someone will show you where you will work. You probably will be given some work to do. If you are not sure what you are supposed to do, ask questions. It is much better to ask lots of questions than to do the work incorrectly.

5. You may be asked to fill out several forms. These forms might include tax forms for the state and U.S. government. You might not have some of the information with you. Ask to take the forms home. Bring the completed forms to work the next day.

The Employee Handbook

You will probably be given an **employee handbook.** This book describes company rules and job benefits. It might also explain what each department does. You do not have to remember all of this information, but you should look through the handbook. Notice the kinds of information in it. Then when you have a question, you will know where to look for the answer. Keep the handbook on your desk or where you do your work so you can find it easily.

Some rules in employee handbooks tell what to do if you are sick and cannot come to work. The rule might be to call your supervisor as soon as possible. Another rule might say that you cannot smoke anywhere in the building.

▶ **Everyday Tip**
Pay attention to the safety rules posted at every job you have.

SAFETY · RULES

- Keep your work area clean.
- Wear safety goggles at all times.
- Do not wear any loose clothing or jewelry.
- Stay alert.

Thank you.

Safety rules are important to know and follow.

Most companies have policies about using the phone. Your handbook should explain when you are allowed to make personal calls. For example, you can make personal phone calls during your breaks or lunchtime. You cannot make them during work hours.

Company rules can also explain the kinds of clothes to wear to work. For example, you may not be allowed to wear jeans, shorts, halter tops, or sandals to work.

Breaking or not following company rules could result in losing your job. You could be **fired**, or dismissed from your job. Then you might have a hard time getting another job. Because of this, it is important to know and follow all the rules in the company handbook.

Did You Know
The term *dress code* describes a company's policy on what employees can wear. In some places, you can be fired from your job if you ignore the dress code.

Practice

A restaurant wants to make an employee handbook. Write five rules for this handbook. You might list the working hours and vacation days. You might tell when employees can take breaks or whether they can have snacks at their work areas. Share your rules with the class.

12-2 ▸ Keeping Your Job

It is usually not difficult to keep a job. All you have to do is be responsible, follow rules and instructions, and have a good attitude. Those three things will make you a valuable employee at any company.

Responsible employees come to work on time every day. They work hard, and they always try to find better ways to do their jobs. They do not take long breaks, make personal phone calls, or waste company time.

When something needs to be done, responsible employees do it, even if it is not their job. They do make mistakes, but they do not make excuses for them. Instead, they find ways to fix whatever they did wrong.

Most employees have supervisors who guide their work. Listen to your supervisor and follow his or her instructions. As you learn your job, you might think of better ways to do it. Some supervisors welcome new ideas. They may want to hear yours.

Other supervisors think their own ideas are best. Think carefully before you suggest changes to this kind of supervisor. Make sure you show a great deal of respect for his or her ideas.

Good employees also have good attitudes. They do not put down the company, its products, or other employees. They do not gossip. They know that people get into disagreements when they work together. However, they find peaceful ways to settle these disagreements. That way, no one ends up angry.

Employees with good attitudes are willing to learn new skills. They know these skills will help them do a better job. When they are asked to do something a different way, they do not insist that the old way is better. They try the new way.

Getting Along at Work

You may like some supervisors and some employees better than others. Still, you must try to get along with everyone. Good communication skills can help. Good communicators are able to share their ideas and opinions without annoying others. They are also good listeners. Good listening helps them understand other people's points of view. When you know what others think and care about, it is easier to get along with them.

Think About It

How can the ability to settle your conflicts peacefully help you get along at work?

Even with good communication skills, getting along with the people at work can be difficult. Sometimes you may wonder what you should say. You may even wonder to whom you should say it. Just remember to show respect to everyone. Treat others as you would like to be treated.

Solving Problems at Work

Even if you respect your co-workers and treat them fairly, you will still face some difficult decisions. Below are some problems that you may face someday. Keep reading to find out how you can solve them by making wise decisions and communicating well.

Suppose something a co-worker is doing is causing a problem for you. For example, suppose a co-worker mixes paint in large cans. Then you stack the cans on shelves. You notice that some lids are not closed tightly. Paint is leaking out of these cans.

You must decide what to do about the problem. You could try to solve the problem yourself. You could try to tighten the paint-can lids. Another option you have is to tell your co-worker about the problem and ask him or her to fix it. You could also discuss the problem with your supervisor.

If you are not sure how to tighten the lids, do not try it. If you are busy, you might not have time to fix the lids. You might also be worried that if you go straight to your supervisor, your co-worker may be angry with you.

Remember

To settle a conflict, listen to each other's point of view. Then work together to think of ways to solve the problem.

The only other choice is to point the problem out to your co-worker. It is important to fix the problem. Be careful not to accuse your co-worker of causing the problem on purpose. Instead, you could say, "Did you notice that some of these lids are not on tight?"

Your co-worker should be glad you pointed out the problem. Now he or she can fix it. However, the co-worker may do nothing. Then you should discuss the problem with your supervisor.

Tell your supervisor that the lids have not been put on correctly. Your supervisor will tell you what to do.

Do not mention that your co-worker ignored you when you pointed out the problem. "Tattling" can get you in deep trouble with your co-workers.

Another problem you might face at work is gossip. Suppose one co-worker mentions that another worker is always late for work. Or a co-worker says that another worker's new haircut looks awful.

You should avoid gossiping. Bad feelings can grow between co-workers because of gossip. Try to avoid conversations that might turn into gossip sessions. You could say, "I didn't notice." You could walk away or get very busy with your work. Any of these responses might discourage the co-worker from more gossiping.

▶ **Everyday Tip**
Treat others the way you would want to be treated.

Practice

Read what each co-worker says below. Then think of a good way you could respond. Write your ideas on another sheet of paper.

1. "I don't care if the paint is leaking out of the cans. It's not my problem."

2. "Come outside with me. I'm going to take a nice long break. It's against company rules, but we can hide behind the building."

3. "We have the worst supervisor! Nothing is ever good enough for him!"

12-3 ▸ Dealing With Customers

If your job involves dealing with customers, you may face many other problems. Part of your job is to keep customers happy. Customers who are not happy will not come back. They may also complain to your supervisor about you.

Suppose you deliver flowers for a florist. What should you do if a customer says, "I don't want these flowers"? This is a challenge for your communication skills. You need to find out politely why the customer is not happy.

You might say, "I'd be glad to take them back. Is there a reason you don't want them?" Then the customer might say, "These aren't the kind of flowers I ordered." Taking the time to communicate allows you to learn more about the problem. Getting more information helps you solve any problem.

Practice

Think of times when you have shopped at a store or eaten in a restaurant. List three things that you like clerks and waiters to do to keep you happy. Then list three things that you do not like them to do. Share your lists with the class.

12-4 Learning New Skills

The more skills you have, the better you can do your job. Suppose your job involves working with a computer. Classes or courses on new computer programs may help you do your job better. Watch for flyers and newspaper articles describing these courses. Choose courses that will help you at work.

Every job offers new learning opportunities.

You can also learn new skills outside the classroom. Suppose you have a new job sorting mail and you work from 9:00 A.M. until 3:00 P.M. After one week, you are able to sort all the mail by 1:00 P.M. You have two hours with nothing to do. Ask your supervisor to show you how to do other tasks. Maybe you could learn how to prepare packages that the company is mailing out. Your supervisor will be impressed that you want to gain more skills. Over time, you could earn a promotion.

Practice

Choose one of the jobs below. Then think of new skills someone with that job could learn from a co-worker. One skill for each job is done for you. Write two more.

1. Mowing lawns for a landscaping company.
   Learning how to plant flowers and trees.

2. Cleaning cages at a pet shop.
   Learning what and how to feed the pets.

3. Washing dishes at a restaurant.
   Learning how to prepare some menu items.

4. Shelving books at the community library.
   Checking out books for customers.

12-5 Following a Schedule

Keeping to a **schedule** is a very important part of any job. A schedule is a list of times to do things. For example, at work you will have a time to start and a time to stop.

Many companies just expect you to arrive and leave work at certain times. At some companies, you might be asked to keep track of the hours you work by writing them on a time sheet.

A time clock records the time each employee starts and stops working.

Using Technology

Many companies today use computerized time clocks to track employees' time.

Other companies use a time clock. Each employee has a time card next to the time clock. The card is slipped into a slot in the time clock. The clock prints the time on your card. When you leave work, you do the same thing. This way, the company has a record of the time you started working and the time you stopped.

Some workplaces have scheduled meal times and break times. Supervisors set up the schedules so some employees are working while others take a break or eat. Remember to punch your time clock when taking breaks and eating meals if that is the company's policy.

If you work at a place that stays open 24 hours a day, you might work a certain **shift.** A shift is a period of time for work. The morning shift might be 7:00 A.M. to 3:00 P.M. The night shift might be 11:00 P.M. to 7:00 A.M. People work shifts at hospitals, police stations, nursing homes, some stores, and other places.

Meeting Deadlines

You might have **deadlines** at work. A deadline is the latest time something can be done. If you work in a mail room, you might have to deliver all the mail by 1:00 P.M. If you work in a restaurant, you might have to set all the tables for dinner by 4:30 P.M.

Think About It

Why is it important to finish a task before the deadline?

Employees who can follow schedules and meet deadlines are valuable. Employees who are often late and miss deadlines might get fired. Those people may have a hard time getting another job.

If your company has shifts, you will need to be flexible. Some businesses are open around the clock. So, someone has to work at night. You may be asked to work nights.

Practice

On a separate sheet of paper, compare a work schedule to a school schedule. List two ways they are alike and two ways they are different.

12-6 ▶ Working Well on a Team

When you work with other people, you are part of a team. Certain qualities make you a valuable member of that team. Team members listen to each other and respect each others' opinions. Teams can get more done when their members have different ideas and skills. Some team members may be good at planning, while others might be better at solving problems. If you know this, it will be easy to respect what each person brings to the team.

Sharing tasks is an important part of working together. All team members need to do their share of the work. Although each person may have different tasks, each should do what he or she does best.

Take pride in your work. This pride will show in your finished product, whatever it is.

The Facts of Life

Sometimes, through no fault of your own, you lose your job. You might be working hard and doing everything right. However, you and many of your co-workers could be victims of a **layoff.** A layoff is a period of time when a company has no work for certain employees. Sometimes a layoff lasts only a few months. Other times you may lose a job forever to a layoff.

Layoffs occur for different reasons. Suppose a company decides to move from Chicago to Atlanta. They might lay off all the workers in Chicago and hire new workers in Atlanta. Suppose a product you are working on is not selling very well. The company might decide to stop making the product and close down your department, or they might decide to sell the part of the company that makes that product. In either case, you would lose your job. It would not matter how hard you had worked.

If you lose your job because of a layoff, you may feel upset or even angry. But there are several things you can do. First, do not feel guilty. Losing your job was not your fault. Second, think of your job as a learning experience. Now you have more experience to add to your résumé. Update your résumé and practice your job interviewing skills. If possible, take some classes to improve your job skills.

Finally, while looking for a new job, you might do temporary work. Temporary workers fill in when regular workers are sick, are on vacation, or have left suddenly. Temporary work is a good way to get more work experience. A company you work for as a "temp" might see that you are a good worker. Then you might be offered a full-time job with the company.

Using Technology

Keep your résumé on a floppy disk or on your computer's hard drive. You can update it quickly and easily.

Practice

Suppose you were laid off. On a separate sheet of paper, list three things you could do to find a new job.

Read the problem below. Then follow the steps to decide which choice is the best solution.

Immanuel works with another person in the mailroom of a large company. His co-worker brings over letters from a printer, checks them, and hands them to Immanuel. Then Immanuel folds each letter and puts it in an envelope. One day Immanuel notices a big ink blot on a letter. He tells his co-worker, "Be careful! I just found a letter with an ink blot."

Immanuel's co-worker says, "Then don't look at the letters. That's not your job."

What should Immanuel do? On a separate sheet of paper, follow the steps below to decide how to handle this problem.

STEP 1 Identify the decision Immanuel must make.

STEP 2 List Immanuel's choices.

STEP 3 Cross out any choices that are harmful or might be against Immanuel's beliefs.

STEP 4 Think about the possible results of each remaining choice.

STEP 5 Select the best choice.

STEP 6 Explain how Immanuel would carry out that choice.

STEP 7 Describe how this decision might affect Immanuel's job.

Make a Difference

What "I message" could Immanuel share with his co-worker?

Summary

Many new employees are nervous on their first day of work. They just need to try to do their best.
On the first day of work, employees are introduced to co-workers and shown where they will work. They usually fill out forms and receive an employee handbook.
To keep your job, you need to be responsible, follow the rules and instructions, and have a good attitude.
Good communication and problem-solving skills can help you get along with others on the job.
Learning new skills at work helps you do a better job. It also shows your supervisor that you are a good worker.
Good employees know how to follow schedules and meet deadlines.
Good employees are good team members. They respect their co-workers, cooperate with them, and take pride in their work.

Vocabulary Review

employee handbook

co-workers

schedule

fired

shift

layoff

deadline

Complete each sentence with a term from the list. Use a separate sheet of paper.

1. A list of times to do things is called a ____.

2. The latest time something can be done is a ____.

3. People who work for the same company are ____.

4. A book that describes company rules and job benefits is an ____.

5. A period of time for work is a ____.

6. If you are dismissed from a job, you are ____.

7. A period of time when a company has no work for employees is a ____.

Chapter Quiz

Write your answers in complete sentences.

1. What can you do to make your first day at work go smoothly?

2. You want to know how many vacation days you will have after you work for a year. How could you find out?

3. What are some reasons that companies make rules?

4. What are three ways to make yourself a valuable employee?

5. What are some ways to be responsible at work?

6. What is one problem-solving skill that is important at work?

7. **CRITICAL THINKING** Sergio's supervisor asked him to learn how to take inventory. Sergio said "No" because he was too busy with the work he already had. Was this a mistake? Why or why not?

Writing Activity

Sometimes a business does not make enough money to pay its employees. When this happens, it may have to lay off some people. Deciding which people to lay off is difficult. Think of at least four ways to choose which employees must lose their jobs. Write them in a list on a separate sheet of paper.

Group Activity

Work with a small group to think of a difficult situation that could happen at work. Then plan a short skit that shows a good way to handle this situation. Write down the dialogue. Act out your skit for the class.

Your first job will probably not be your lifetime job. Still, it is a good place to start thinking about your career goals. What can you learn from your first job?

Learning Objectives

- Identify what to consider in setting a specific, realistic, long-term career goal.
- Describe how to set up a career plan to meet that goal.
- Name some ways to gain an employer's trust.
- Explain how to handle a job review.
- Describe how to ask for a raise or promotion.

Chapter 13 — Making the Most of a Job

Words to Know

career goal the work you would like to be doing several years from now

career plan a step-by-step way to reach a career goal

promotion a new job with more responsibility and more pay

job review a rating of how well you are doing on your job

Getting and keeping a job are important achievements. Kaylee was starting to wonder about her job. Read the story below to find out what was bothering Kaylee.

> Kaylee liked her job serving customers at a fast-food restaurant. The work was pleasant, and her friends often stopped by. The manager didn't mind if she talked to them, as long as she got her work done.
>
> Lately, Kaylee had begun to wonder what she would be doing when she got older. She wondered whether she would still be working at that restaurant.
>
> Kaylee worked hard. Her job kept her on her feet all day. She did not think she would want to stand up all day when she got older. Even now, Kaylee's legs ached by the end of the day.
>
> "Maybe," Kaylee thought, "I should be thinking about my future and a different job."

Once you have learned how to get and keep a job, it is time to look ahead. It is time to think about a career.

It is best to think about your personal qualities, skills, and interests before you look for a job. That way, you will be more likely to find a job that suits you. However, it is also important to consider your job needs right now. For example, you may want a job that pays you enough money to buy a car, or you might need a job that will fit into your schedule.

At some point, you will need a job that pays you enough money to meet all your basic needs. So, like Kaylee, you must plan further ahead. You should think about what you will need five or ten years from now.

Consider setting a **career goal**. A career goal is the work you would like to be doing several years from now. Setting a career goal gives you something to aim for in your future.

Think About It

What can you do right now to start working on a career goal?

Deciding what you want to do with your life takes some thought. You still need to consider your personal qualities, skills, interests, and needs. You should choose a job that suits you. However, your career goal might require skills that you do not have right now. You can start learning those skills, once you have chosen your goal.

To set a career goal, think of what you want from a job. Do not limit yourself to what you want right now. Think about what you might want in the future. For example, maybe you want to help others. Your career goal might be to become an X-ray technician. Maybe you want to have your own business, and you like working with cars. Your career goal might be to open a car repair shop.

Being Realistic and Specific

A career goal needs to be realistic. Many people would like to be famous actors, athletes, or musicians. However, these are not very realistic goals for most people. You can still try to be a professional actor, athlete, or musician, but you also need other, more realistic goals. It is important to work on realistic goals at all times. You can always set bigger goals later on.

Evan had been thinking about being a physical therapist. He learned he would need some special training. The training would include several science courses. Science had not been one of his favorite subjects. He would have to work very hard to improve his science grades. To make sure he wanted to be a physical therapist, Evan decided to take a related job first. He decided to try a job as an assistant trainer. He could work in a gym or health club. That job would help him decide whether he really wanted to be a physical therapist.

A career goal should also be specific. Candace set a goal of working in Florida within two years. This goal would be easy to reach. However, it is not specific enough. Her goal does not describe the kind of work she can do.

> **Did You Know ?**
> Some careers require many years of training. When you set a career goal, you should consider the training you will need.

Practice

The goals below were written by students who had just graduated from high school. Decide which goals are realistic and specific. Write your answers on a separate sheet of paper.

1. In three years, I want to be the star of a television comedy show.

2. In two years, I want to be a home health aide and set my own work hours.

3. By the end of this year, I want to get a job where I supervise at least ten people.

4. In five years, I want to be a carpenter and own my own tools.

After you choose a specific and realistic career goal, you need a **career plan.** A career plan is a step-by-step way to reach a career goal.

First, write down your career goal. Choose a job that fits your personal qualities, skills, interests, and needs. Make sure the goal is specific and realistic.

Next, list the steps to reach your goal. For example, Kaylee decided to work toward a goal of owning her own flower shop. She thought the best way to start working toward her goal was to learn about plants and flowers. Her next step was to get a job in a flower shop. Once she began working at the shop, she could learn from her co-workers about flower arranging. She could learn how to order plants and supplies and how to keep on a budget. Most importantly, she would learn how to keep customers happy. Kaylee also decided that she would take courses to learn more about the business. While she was learning the business, Kaylee could save money to buy her own flower shop.

▶ **Everyday Tip**
Start learning the skills you need to reach your career goal.

Kaylee realized that she had to follow some rules while she worked toward her goal. She also knew how important it is to be responsible. Then her supervisor would put her in charge of other workers. That is how Kaylee would learn to supervise her own employees.

Your career plan will help you identify the steps you need to take. You will then know what you have to do to reach your career goal.

Set up a timeline to help move your plans along. Think about how much time each of your steps should take. You might measure this time in months or years. For instance, Kaylee might work at a flower shop for seven years before buying her own shop. Remember, this timeline is just a guess. Many things can affect it. You may complete a step sooner or later than you planned.

You might need to add a step. As you work toward your goal, you might even skip a step.

Identifying any obstacles that could stop you from reaching your goal is important. Things can get in the way of meeting your goal. For example, Kaylee might have trouble saving enough money to buy her own shop. However, she might think of a way to overcome this problem. She could ask two of her friends to be her partners. Then they could help her buy the shop.

Write down any obstacles you might face. Then name some ways you could overcome each obstacle.

Identify sources of help that you can use when you need to overcome obstacles. Decide who or what can help you reach your goal. You may think of supervisors, co-workers, or even customers who could help you. Kaylee's friends, for example, might be sources of help for her.

Learning a new skill can help you reach your career goal.

Check your progress as you work toward a goal. Make any changes in your plan that you think will help you move closer to reaching your goal.

As you get closer to your goal, you may already have a new goal. Add it to your career plan.

Practice

Talk with two people who have successful careers. They might be family members, neighbors, or staff at school. These people do not have to earn lots of money. They should just be happy with their work. That is success!

Ask them to explain the steps they took to get where they are now. Then draw stair steps on a separate sheet of paper. Write the steps each person took toward his or her goal.

13-3 ▶ Working Toward Your Career Goal

Remember
Learning new skills at work can help you do a better job.

Suppose your career goal is to be a toy designer. As your first step, you get a job in a toy factory. Your job is to put wheels on toy trucks. One day your supervisor offers you a **promotion**. A promotion is a new job with more responsibility and more pay.

However, in this new job you would not be designing toys. You would be selling them. You would travel around the country and show the company's toys to toy stores.

The problem with the promotion is that this sales job is not part of your career plan. You must decide what to do. As with all decisions, you need to think about the possible results of each choice. If you took the job selling toys, you would earn more money. You would also get to travel. However, you might not be working toward your goal of being a toy designer.

You can decide to take a job that is not in your original career plan. You need to be flexible so you can take advantage of new opportunities. A job in sales could take you in an interesting direction. It might also help you meet your career goal. By selling toys, you might get ideas for new toys. You could take those ideas back to your company. Maybe you could design the new toys.

Earning Trust

Setting a career goal is important. It helps you plan where you are going in the future. However, you also need to make the most of any job, even if it is not part of your plan. To do that, you must earn your employer's trust.

When your employer trusts you, you will be more likely to get promotions and raises. When your employer knows you are responsible, you may be allowed to make more of your own decisions. Your employer may realize that you do not need to be closely supervised.

You must show an employer that you can be trusted. Suppose you have been working for a delivery company. You ride with a driver and help him load and unload a small truck. One morning, this driver does not show up for work. Your supervisor needs another driver immediately. You volunteer to drive. You tell the supervisor you know you can do it. He takes a chance and gives you the driver's schedule. You follow it carefully and do a good job.

The next time your supervisor needs a driver, he might ask you first. You have proven that you can be trusted. Soon you might have your own truck to drive. However, it takes time to gain an employer's trust. It is your employer's decision when to give you a promotion, not yours. You cannot demand more responsibility or a promotion.

▶ **Everyday Tip**
Do not ignore interesting new opportunities. You might change your career goal as your interests and needs change.

Every job has opportunities to show that you are trustworthy.

There are certain guidelines that can help you gain your employer's trust. Be reliable and responsible on the job all the time, not just in front of a supervisor. Prove that people can count on you. Always be on time. Always do a little more than what is required in your job. Do not make excuses for your mistakes. Instead, fix them.

Another guideline to follow on the job is to stay flexible. Offer to change your schedule and help out in emergencies. Be willing to try new ways of doing things. Being flexible is another way of being cooperative.

Remember to be visible and confident. Let your supervisor see you and your work. Take pride in your work. Show that you know you can do the job. Ask to take on new duties. Then handle them well. Look for opportunities to prove yourself.

Practice

Think about a job you would like to have. What could you do on this job to gain your supervisor's trust? Write your ideas on a separate sheet of paper.

13-4 Handling Job Reviews

After you have worked for several months, your supervisor may give you a **job review.** A job review is a rating of how well you are doing your job. The supervisor will describe what you are doing right. He or she will also explain what you need to improve. You will probably receive your job review in a meeting with your supervisor and also in writing.

As part of your job review, you might receive a score for each responsibility you have at work. The responsibilities listed on your job review will depend on your job. For example, if you work as part of a team, you might be rated on how well you cooperate with team members.

During a job review, your supervisor will list your strong points. Remember these and continue to do them well. It is also important to listen carefully to learn what your supervisor thinks you need to improve. Try not to argue or give excuses. Show that you are eager and willing to improve.

Asking for a Raise or Promotion
A job review sometimes includes a promotion or a raise. This means that some people receive a raise or promotion without asking for it. However, many do not receive a promotion or raise during a job review.

Think About It

How can you use the information from your job review to improve your job performance?

If you think you deserve a better job or more pay, find out about your company's policy. You might look for this information in your employee handbook. You could call the human resources or personnel department.

If you want to ask for a promotion or raise, meet with your employer. Explain why you think you deserve it. By asking, you show you are confident of your skills. In the end, however, it is the supervisor's decision whether to give you a raise or promotion.

Getting Ahead

Make the most of any job. Set a career goal and work toward it. To get ahead where you work now, show that you can do the job. Work hard. Earn good reviews. Then maybe promotions and raises will follow.

Practice

Ask someone who works full-time the questions below. Write the answers on a separate sheet of paper.

1. How would someone at your company get a raise or promotion?

2. What qualities have helped people to be promoted?

Read about the problem below. Then follow the steps to help Ted decide what to do.

Ted has been working in a restaurant for a month. He is a kitchen helper and cleans up after the chef. One evening Ted forgot about a large plate of chicken that the chef had prepared. When he got to work the next day, Ted found the chicken. It had been on the counter all night. Now it was probably spoiled. No one should eat it.

Just then the chef came in. She asked Ted to get the chicken out of the refrigerator. She was going to make chicken salad. Ted wants the chef to trust him.

On a separate sheet of paper, follow the steps below to help Ted decide what to do.

STEP 1   Identify the decision Ted must make.

STEP 2   List Ted's choices.

STEP 3   Cross out any choices that are harmful or might be against Ted's beliefs.

STEP 4   Think about the possible results of each remaining choice.

STEP 5   Select the best choice.

STEP 6   Explain how Ted would carry out that choice.

STEP 7   Describe the possible results.

Make a Difference

What would you suggest Ted tell the chef?

Summary

One way to make the most of your job is to set a long-term career goal. Setting a career goal can give you something to work toward.

Your career goal should be realistic and specific. It should take into account your personal qualities, skills, interests, and needs.

Setting up a step-by-step career plan can help you reach your career goal.

To get ahead at work, means you must earn an employer's trust. You earn trust when you are reliable, responsible, flexible, visible, and confident in your own abilities.

Job reviews help employees learn about their strengths and weaknesses. You should continue actions that are considered strengths. Work to improve your skills in any areas in which you have weaknesses.

One day you might want to ask for a raise or a promotion. Find out when the company gives them. Or, politely ask your supervisor for a raise or a promotion. Do not be discouraged if you do not get it. Try again later.

Vocabulary Review

career plan

job review

promotion

career goal

Write the term from the list that matches each definition below. Use a separate sheet of paper.

1. a rating of how well you are doing on your job

2. a step-by-step way to reach a career goal

3. the work you would like to be doing several years from now

4. a new job with more responsibility and more pay

Chapter Quiz

Write your answers in complete sentences.

1. What are some things to consider when you set a career goal?

2. Renata's career goal is to earn $25,000 a year. Is this a good career goal? Why or why not?

3. What are the steps in creating a career plan?

4. What are some ways to gain a supervisor's trust?

5. How should you respond to a job review?

6. Your department is facing a major deadline. One employee is out sick. Is this a good time to ask for a raise or a promotion? Why or why not?

7. **CRITICAL THINKING** After you set a career goal, should you stick to it, no matter what? Why or why not?

Writing Activity

Job reviews usually become part of each employee's work record. What if you thought your job review was unfair? Maybe you received a low score in an area in which you think you do well. What might you do? Write a paragraph about it on a separate sheet of paper.

Group Activity

For the third summer, Elizabeth worked as a camp lifeguard. The camp director needed a new supervisor. Elizabeth knew she could handle the job. However, the camp director did not seem to be considering her. Have each member of a small group list two ways Elizabeth could get the job. Discuss your ideas. Then write a letter to Elizabeth telling her some of your ideas. Wish her well.

Unit 4 **Review**

Read each sentence below. Then choose the letter that best completes each one.

1. Before you look for a job, consider all of the following, except
   A. your personal qualities.
   B. your friend's interests.
   C. your skills.
   D. your interests.

2. A good place to look for a new job is
   A. in the phone book.
   B. in the "Want Ads" section of a newspaper.
   C. on neighborhood bulletin boards.
   D. all of the above

3. The best way to handle a job review is
   A. think of how you can improve.
   B. listen closely, then leave.
   C. criticize your employer.
   D. discuss it with co-workers.

4. When you set a long-term career goal, you
   A. think ahead to next month.
   B. do not follow a career plan.
   C. plan what skills you need to learn for the future.
   D. all of the above

5. An employee handbook often tells you about
   A. government policies.
   B. rates of pay for everyone in the company.
   C. worker benefits in the United States.
   D. company departments and what they do.

6. One thing good employees do is
   A. work for themselves, not for the team.
   B. follow directions from time to time.
   C. cooperate with their co-workers.
   D. leave work before the assigned time.

7. When you are at a job interview, you should
   A. look the other person in the eye.
   B. speak as quickly as possible.
   C. stand while speaking.
   D. never ask questions.

Critical Thinking

What are good communication skills? How can they help you get along with people at work?

WRITING Write a short essay telling how to find out what jobs are available in your community. Include whether you have tried to get a job or have gotten a job using any of the sources.

Unit 5 ▷ Handling Your Money

It is a good idea to choose a bank that offers the services you need and has a branch near your home. What kinds of bank services do you think you will need?

Learning Objectives

- Describe a checking account.
- Explain how to open and use a checking account.
- Explain how to fill out a deposit slip, check, and check register.
- Describe how to open and use a savings account.
- Explain the importance of keeping track of money in a checking or savings account.
- Identify issues to consider when choosing a bank.

Words to Know

checking account	a bank account from which a depositor can withdraw money using a check or a debit card
deposit	money put in a bank account
check	a written order directing a bank to pay a certain amount of money from the account of the person who signs it to the person named
minimum	the lowest amount of money a depositor can keep in an account without being charged an additional fee
interest	money that a bank pays you for keeping your money in that bank
ATM	an automatic teller machine; a machine that allows you to take money out of or put money into your bank account using a special card
signature card	a card you sign when you open a bank account
deposit slip	a form you fill out that shows how much money you are putting in the bank
receipt	a form that the bank gives you that shows how much money you put in or took out of your bank account
check register	a small chart where you record the checks you write and the deposits you make
balance	the amount of money in a bank account
savings account	a bank account on which interest is paid and from which a depositor can withdraw money
withdrawal slip	a form used to take money out of the bank
bank statement	a report that the bank sends you to show how much money is in your accounts

Some banks charge an extra fee if the money in your checking account falls below a certain amount. This fee is called a minimum balance charge. Another fee could be a check printing fee. Checks must be printed with your name and address on each check. Some banks charge a fee for printing these checks. Other banks do not. Some banks charge a fee of $.50 to $1.00 for each check you write. Others do not.

A bank may also charge a monthly or yearly fee just to keep your account open. Again, there may be no fee if you keep a certain amount of money in your account.

Another common bank charge is a fee each time customers use an **ATM**, or automatic teller machine. ATMs are machines that allow you to take money out of or put money into your bank account using a special card. ATMs are often located at banks, shopping malls, bus stations, supermarkets, and other public places.

Banks may also offer other services. Make sure you understand how much a bank charges for each of its services. Once you add up all the fees each bank charges, you can decide which is the best bank for you.

Practice

With a partner, visit a nearby bank. Find out what fees it charges for checking accounts. Write them down. Share what you learn with the class. Discuss which nearby banks offer the lowest fees for checking accounts.

14-2 ▸ Opening a Checking Account

To open a checking account, you must prove who you are. When you go to the bank, take identification with you. It should be something with your name, address, picture, and signature on it. You might use your driver's license or your school ID.

Some banks require proof of where you live. They may ask for a piece of mail that you received at your home address. When you go to open any account, take with you two letters or bills that you got in the mail. Try to use mail that is no more than one year old. The bank wants to make sure your address is valid.

You will also need your birthdate, Social Security number, and phone number. You might need a minimum deposit to open the account. Find out the amount ahead of time. Then take enough cash with you to open your account.

If you are less than 18 years old, the bank might put the account in your name and a parent's name. This means that both of you can put money into the account and take it out.

When you open your account, you will sign a **signature card.** This card shows the bank how you sign your name. Later, bank employees can check this card to make sure you are the one who signed your checks.

Filling Out a Deposit Slip

When you open a checking account, you will fill out a **deposit slip.** This form shows how much money you are putting in your account. Every time you put money in the bank, you will fill out a deposit slip.

Carrie Davis	CASH CURRENCY	$10 00
12 East Broadway Street	COIN	
Galloway, Illinois 12345	LIST CHECKS SINGLY	$139 80
DATE July 23, 2001		
DEPOSITS MAY NOT BE AVAILABLE FOR IMMEDIATE WITHDRAWAL		55-555/1234 7654321
Carrie Davis		
SIGN HERE FOR CASH RECEIVED (IF REQUIRED)	TOTAL	$149 80
First Street Bank	LESS CASH RECEIVED	
102 First Street	NET DEPOSIT	$149 80
Galloway, Illinois 12345		BE SURE EACH ITEM IS PROPERLY ENDORSED

DEPOSIT TICKET · PLEASE PRESS FIRMLY

⑈⦂087123528⦂⦂ 0823103⑈ 34

CHECKS AND OTHER ITEMS ARE RECEIVED FOR DEPOSIT SUBJECT TO THE PROVISIONS OF THE UNIFORM COMMERCIAL CODE OR ANY APPLICABLE COLLECTION AGREEMENT.

A deposit slip shows how much money you are putting into your bank account.

Look at the deposit slip on page 195. Carrie filled this out when she opened her checking account. She listed her paycheck for $139.80 in the space that says "List Checks Singly." She also listed the $10 bill she was depositing in the space marked "Cash." Then she added the numbers for the total of $149.80.

When you deposit money, the bank will give you a **receipt.** A receipt is a form that you fill out to show how much money you put into or took out of your account. Make sure the amount shown on the receipt is correct. Save your receipts in a safe place at home. If you have questions about your account later, you can refer back to your receipts.

How to Write a Check

The bank will give you a set of checks. You may have to pay a fee for your checks. You may also have to wait a few days to get checks with your name and address printed on them. Some banks will give you temporary checks to use in the meantime. Look at the check on page 197 that Carrie wrote. Notice the different parts of the check.

Always write checks with a pen, not a pencil. Someone could erase writing in pencil and change what you wrote on your check. Write the date on your check. Carefully and clearly write the name of the person or company that will cash the check.

Be careful when you write the amount of the check in words and in numbers. The two amounts must be the same. Remember to fill the entire amount line when you write the amount of the check in words. Start writing at the left end of the line. If there is space left over, fill it with a line. That makes it harder for anyone to change the amount you wrote on the check. If you make a mistake, tear up the check. Write a new check. The bank might not cash your check if it has any crossed-out mistakes.

Using Technology

Many banks allow customers access to their account information on the Internet. It is available 24 hours a day.

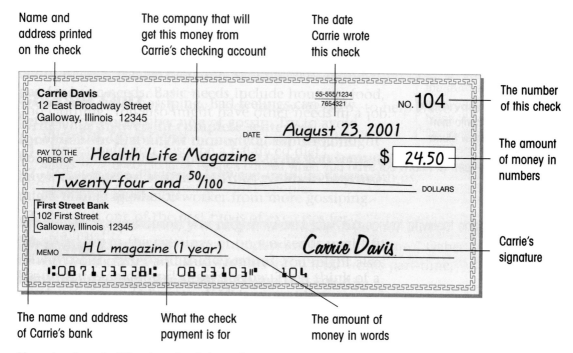

Knowing how to fill out a check is an important skill.

Never sign a blank check. Someone could fill in the check with his or her own name and any amount of money. Also, if someone uses your checks you could lose all the money in your checking account. Never lend your checks to anyone. Even if someone else writes the check and signs it, the money will come out of your checking account.

Always sign your name the way you signed your signature card. Suppose a person signed his name as "Jeremy" on his signature card. He should not sign a check "Jerry." If he does, the bank might not accept the signature on the check. It might not get cashed.

Practice

Answer these questions on a separate sheet of paper.

1. Where is Carrie's name on the check? Does it appear in more than one place? Why?

2. What bank name is on the check? Why is it written there?

3. How much money is the check for?

4. To whom is the check written?

14-3 ▶ Keeping Track of Your Money

Every time you write a check, you must record it in a **check register.** A check register is a small chart where you record the checks you write and the deposits you make. It is part of your checkbook. Look at Carrie's check register below. See how she recorded a deposit and a check.

Notice the part of the check register marked **balance.** The balance is the amount of money in a checking account. Every time you write a check or make a deposit, your balance changes. When you write a check, you must subtract that amount from your balance. When you make a deposit, you must add that amount to your

		PLEASE BE SURE TO DEDUCT ANY CHECK CHARGES OR SERVICE CHARGES THAT MAY APPLY TO YOUR ACCOUNT						
NUMBER	DATE	DESCRIPTION OF TRANSACTION	(-) PAYMENT		FEE (IF ANY)	(+) DEPOSIT	BALANCE $	
	7/23/01	Deposit				149 80	149 80	
							149 80	
104	8/23/01	Health Life Magazine	24 50				24 50	
							125 30	

A check register is a chart where you record the checks you write and the deposits you make.

balance. Then you will know exactly how much money is in your checking account.

When you deposit a check, it must clear before you can use the money. For a check to clear, there must be enough money in the account of the person who wrote it to cover the amount of the check. That money is then put into your account.

▶ **Everyday Tip**
Enter your bank deposits and withdrawals as soon as possible. This way you always know exactly how much money you have in your account.

Suppose that Carrie started her checking account by depositing $149.80. Carrie's balance was $149.80. When she wrote a check to pay for a magazine subscription, she subtracted it from her balance. $149.80 − $24.50 = $125.30. Her new balance is $125.30.

Carrie should not write a check for more than $125.30. That is all the money she has in her checking account right now.

Practice

Answer the questions below on a separate sheet of paper. Use the check register on page 198.

1. What was Carrie's starting balance in her checking account?

2. Why did Carrie's balance change to $125.30?

3. If Carrie deposits another paycheck for $149.80, what will her new balance be?

14-4 ▶ Choosing a Bank

You could keep all your money in your wallet. Then you could pay cash whenever you bought something. Cash is paper money and coins. However, your wallet could get lost or stolen. Then your cash would be gone. Putting your money in a bank is much safer. Your money will be safe there until you take it out or write a check.

Suppose you have decided to put your money in a bank. Your community has several banks. Most banks have several offices. You must decide which bank is best for you. Do not choose a bank just because of an ad or because a friend goes there.

First of all, a bank should be easy to visit. Begin your search for a bank by checking the ones near your home or the place where you work. Find out how long they are open every day. Some are open in the evenings. Some are even open on Sundays. The more the bank is open, the easier it will be for you to put money in or take money out.

The next step in choosing a bank is learning about the services it offers. Some banks charge for certain services. Other banks provide the same services for free. Shop around to find out.

Practice

With a partner, list all the banks you know of in your community. Share your list with the class. How many different banks are there? Then look in the phone book to find out how many offices each bank has. List offices that are near your school or job.

14-5 ► Learning How Savings Accounts Work

It is smart for you to save money for things you want. However, if you try to save your money in a drawer at home, you might spend it. If you put your money in a **savings account** at a bank, it would not be so easy to spend. A savings account is a bank account on which interest is paid and from which a depositor can withdraw money.

Banks almost never charge fees for having a savings account. In fact, if you put money in a savings account, you will earn money. All banks must pay interest on savings accounts. It is the law. The interest for a savings account is always higher than the interest for a checking account.

For example, a bank that pays 5 percent interest on a savings account might pay 1 percent interest on a checking account. That means the savings account pays five times more interest than the checking account. If you put $100 in this savings account and left it there, you would earn $5 at the end of a year. However, if you put $100 in this checking account and left it there for a year, you would earn only $1.

The longer you leave money in a savings account, the more interest you will earn. The more money you put in your account, the more interest you will earn.

Think About It

Why would money that is kept in a drawer earn no interest?

You can get money out of your savings account by using your ATM card. You can fill out a **withdrawal slip,** a form used to take money out of the bank. You can also move, or transfer, money from your savings account to your checking account.

However, you probably should not put all your money into a savings account. You cannot write a check on the money in your savings account. Many banks set a limit on how often you can take money out of a savings account. For example, at one bank, you can take money out of a savings account only six times a month without paying a fee. However, you can make deposits in a savings account as often as you like.

Opening and Using a Savings Account

Opening a savings account is like opening a checking account. You have to fill out forms and sign a signature card. You also have to bring a check or cash for the bank's minimum deposit for a savings account.

The bank may give you a small book, called a passbook, in which it will list each deposit and withdrawal. Or you may have a register, like a check register, in which you keep track of your account.

Your savings account will have a balance, just like your checking account. You will have to add your deposits and your interest to your balance. You will have to subtract your withdrawals. Keeping track of a savings account is like keeping track of a checking account.

Banking Benefits

A checking account can help you pay your bills. A savings account can help you save for the future. Both kinds of accounts can be very helpful.

At the end of each month, your bank will send you a **bank statement**. A bank statement is a report that the bank sends you to show how much money is in your accounts. Most banks send a checking account statement at the end of each month. Your checking account statement will list your balance and any checks you wrote and any withdrawals or deposits you made. It will also list any bank fees that have been taken out of your account. Use this information to make sure the balance in your check register is correct.

Most banks also send bank statements to show how much money is in your savings account. Some banks send a statement every month. Other banks send statements every three months. A savings account statement lists your deposits and withdrawals. It also lists the amount of interest you have earned on your savings. You should look at the balance in your savings account register. Remember to add the interest the bank has paid you to the balance in your register.

Learning how to choose and use a bank is another part of preparing to live on your own. If you still have questions, ask a parent or someone else who knows how to use banks.

Practice

Make a list of three ways checking accounts are different from savings accounts.

Read the situation below. Then help Luis decide which bank he should choose—Capital Bank or Branford Bank.

Capital Bank requires customers to keep at least $200 in their checking accounts at all times. If a customer's balance falls below $200, the customer must pay $.75 for each check he or she writes. Luis writes about ten checks a month. He has $350 for his first deposit. However, he will soon have to make a $200 car payment.

At Branford Bank, Luis can keep any amount in his checking account. He does not have to pay a fee for writing checks. However, he will have to pay a service charge of $9 a month on his checking account.

On a separate sheet of paper, follow the steps below. Help Luis decide which bank to choose.

STEP 1   Identify the problem Luis must solve.

STEP 2   List Luis's choices.

STEP 3   Cross out any choices that are harmful or might be against Luis's beliefs.

STEP 4   Think about the possible results of each choice. You will have to do some math for this step.

STEP 5   Select the best choice.

STEP 6   Explain how Luis would carry out this choice.

STEP 7   Describe the possible results of Luis's choice.

Make a Difference

What advice would you give Luis about choosing a bank?

Summary

When you open a checking account, you put money in the bank and then write checks. The bank gives the money to whomever you wrote checks.
Many banks have a minimum deposit for checking and savings accounts.
Banks charge fees for checking and some savings accounts. These could include check fees, service charges, and ATM charges.
When you put money in your account, you need to fill out a deposit slip.
Always fill out checks carefully and clearly using a pen. Also sign and date the check. Never sign a blank check.
Put money you wish to save in a savings account. Banks pay interest on your savings accounts.
A bank statement is a report of how much money is in your account. Use the information to make sure your balance is correct.

Vocabulary Review

signature card

receipt

deposit slip

balance

savings account

withdrawal slip

ATM

Complete each sentence with a term from the box. Use a separate sheet of paper.

1. A card you sign when you open a bank account is a ____.

2. The amount of money in a bank account is the ____.

3. A form used to take money out of the bank is a ____.

4. Money kept in a bank gains interest in a ____.

5. A ____ shows how much money you put in or took out of your account.

6. The abbreviation for "automatic teller machine" is ____.

7. A ____ shows how much money you are putting in the bank.

Chapter Quiz

Write your answers in complete sentences.

1. Tammy wrote a check to a shoe store for $46.78. However, she only has $17.18 in her checking account. What will happen?

2. What is the difference between the interest banks pay and a fee for an account?

3. When you open a checking account, what information do you need to have with you?

4. What are three tips for writing checks?

5. What could happen if you do not keep track of the checks you write?

6. Will your money earn more interest in a checking account or in a savings account? Why?

7. **CRITICAL THINKING** What things should you consider when you choose a bank?

Writing Activity

Most stores charge customers $15 or more if banks return their checks. However, most people are honest. They just do not know how much money is in their checking accounts. Should honest people be charged for writing bad checks? Why or why not? Write your point of view in a paragraph on a separate sheet of paper.

Group Activity

Work with a partner to learn about checking accounts. Each partner will talk with someone who has a checking account. Find out why this person chose that bank. Does the bank pay interest on checking accounts? What fees does it charge for checking accounts? Compare and contrast the information you learn. Make a chart.

Managing your money carefully allows you to buy the things you really want. What are some ways you can manage your money?

Learning Objectives

- Explain the information shown on a paycheck.
- Explain the information on a paycheck stub.
- Describe how to cash a paycheck.
- Describe how to set up a budget.
- Explain why it is important to stay on a budget.
- Identify reasons why people save money.
- Explain how to manage your money.

Chapter 15 Managing Your Money

Words to Know

paycheck	a check from your employer for the money earned from a job
paycheck stub	a form attached to a paycheck that lists important information
gross pay	the total amount of money an employee earns
deduction	money taken out of a paycheck
net pay	the amount of money an employee receives after deductions are taken out of the gross pay
cash a check	to give a check to a bank and receive the amount of money written on it
teller	a bank employee who works behind the counter
endorse	to sign your name on the back of a check
expenses	payments
budget	a plan for spending money
retirement	the years after a person stops working and earning income
Social Security	a government-run retirement savings program

Read the situation below about Keith. He lives at home, earns money, yet does not manage it well.

> When Keith received his first paycheck, he felt rich. He bought a shirt he had wanted for a long time. He went to a couple of movies with friends. He also had pizza after work a few times. After only four days, Keith was broke. "I must have lost some of my money," he said. "I couldn't have spent it all!"

Keith needs to learn how to handle his money so it does not seem to disappear. This chapter will help you learn how to manage your money. Then you will have some when you need it!

15-1 ▶ Understanding Your Paycheck

When you have a job and start earning money, you receive a **paycheck.** A paycheck is a check from your employer. It has your name on it. Your paycheck also shows the amount of money that your employer is paying you for your work.

Some employers pay their employees every week. Other employers pay them every two weeks. Still others pay employees only once a month.

The amount of money in your paycheck depends on several things. It may be based on how much money you earn per hour and the number of hours you worked. Other types of paychecks are based on a set amount for a certain job.

Keith's paycheck is for $85.30. That is how much he earned for the hours he worked last week. Keith works at Grant's Grocery Store. This store keeps its money at

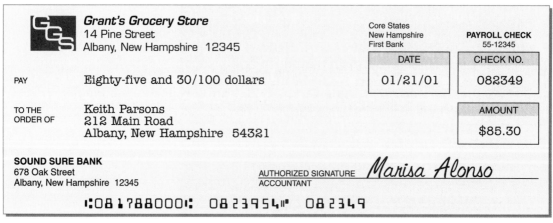

This is a paycheck. You may receive a paycheck once a week or once a month.

Sound Sure Bank. That is why Sound Sure Bank is the name printed on the bottom of Keith's paycheck.

The check also shows the date it was written. It was signed by Marisa Alonso. Ms. Alonso works at the store and writes its checks.

Practice

Suppose you worked for Grant's Grocery Store and wrote its checks. On a separate sheet of paper, draw a paycheck. Use a partner's name in place of Keith's. Show $63.25 as the amount your partner is being paid. Write the amount in numbers and in words, as on Keith's paycheck. Sign the paycheck with your name in place of Ms. Alonso's. Show this paycheck to your partner. Discuss whether you put the information in the right places.

15-2 ➤ Understanding a Paycheck Stub

A filled-in form is attached to Keith's paycheck. This is the **paycheck stub.** It lists a great deal of information. When Keith gets his paycheck, he looks at the stub to be sure that it is correct. First, he checks

Grant's Grocery Store

EMPLOYEE NUMBER	CURRENT HOURS		CURRENT				
	REGULAR	OVERTIME	Y.T.D. NET	F.I.T.	F.I.C.A.	STATE TAX	LOCAL TAX
12345	20|00	|00	170|60	18|00	9|00	6|00	1|70

CURRENT EARNINGS			YEAR TO DATE				
REGULAR	OVERTIME	SPECIAL	Y.T.D. GROSS	F.I.T.	F.I.C.A.	STATE TAX	LOCAL TAX
120|00	|00	|00	240|00	36|00	18|00	12|00	3|40

CHECK NO.	DESCRIPTION	AMOUNT	DESCRIPTION	AMOUNT	TOTAL DEDUCTIONS
082349					
ENDING DATE					34|70
01|14|01					
CHECK DATE					NET PAY
01|21|01	AUTHORIZED DEDUCTIONS AND SPECIAL PAY ELEMENTS				85|30

STATEMENT OF EARNINGS AND DEDUCTIONS • DETACH AND RETAIN FOR YOUR RECORDS

This is a paycheck stub.

the "Current Hours" box. He wants to see whether it shows all the hours he worked last week. The "Current Hours" box on this paycheck is correct. It shows that Keith worked 20 hours last week, with no overtime.

Then Keith multiplies the number of hours he worked by his pay for each hour. Keith makes $6 an hour: 20 hours times $6 per hour is $120.00. Keith checks the "Current Earnings" box on his paycheck stub. The amount is correct: $120.00.

The total amount of money an employee earns is called **gross pay.** Look for the "Current Earnings" section on Keith's paycheck stub. It shows $120.00, which is the total amount he earned. That is his gross pay.

But Keith received a check for only $85.30. This is because some money was taken out of his paycheck. Money taken out of a paycheck is called a **deduction.**

Below are the main kinds of deductions. They are listed on Keith's paycheck stub. These deductions are all taxes. Most employees have these deductions taken out of their paychecks. Other paychecks may have other kinds of deductions.

Deductions	
F.I.T.	Federal income tax
F.I.C.A.	Social security tax
State tax	State tax
Local tax	City tax

Each tax is shown twice on Keith's paycheck stub. The "Current" numbers are the total taxes only for this paycheck. The year-to-date (Y.T.D.) numbers are the total taxes he has paid so far this year. The "Total Deductions" box shows all the deductions for this paycheck: $34.70.

The amount of money an employee receives after deductions are taken out of the gross pay is called **net pay.** Find the "Net Pay" box on the paycheck stub. It shows

$85.30. This is the amount of money Keith actually gets to keep. To figure net pay, subtract all deductions from the gross pay: $120.00 − $34.70 = $85.30.

Practice

Answer these questions on a separate sheet of paper.

1. How much money was taken from Keith's paycheck for local taxes? How much has been taken out for local taxes so far this year?

2. What does Y.T.D. Gross mean?

15-3 ▸ Cashing a Paycheck

When you **cash a check**, you give it to a person at a bank or a business that cashes checks. That person gives you the amount of money written on the check. Keith could go to a check-cashing business. However, he knows that he must pay a fee to this business to cash his check.

Keith wants to keep all the money he earned, so he goes to a bank. If he goes to the right bank, he can cash his check free. Keith could go to the bank named on the check. That is Sound Sure Bank. If Keith had his own checking account, he could go to his own bank.

The Sound Sure Bank is near Grant's Grocery Store, so Keith goes there. The bank employee who works behind the counter is called a **teller.** The teller asks to see identification, or something with Keith's picture, signature, and name on it. The teller must be sure he is giving the money to the person whose name is on the check. Keith shows the teller his driver's license. It has his name, picture, and signature on it.

Keith must **endorse** the check. This means he must sign his name on the back of the check. The teller

Think About It

Why is it important to bring identification with you to the bank?

checks Keith's signature against the signature on Keith's driver's license. They look the same, so the teller gives Keith $85.30 in cash. Keith counts the money to make sure it is the right amount before he leaves the bank.

▶ **Everyday Tip**
Always count your money before leaving a bank or ATM machine.

Practice

On a separate sheet of paper, write two reasons why Keith was wise to use the Sound Sure Bank to cash his paycheck.

15-4 ▸ Creating a Budget

Think back to Keith's problem. He spent his money quickly and was unsure of what he had bought. Keith wants to be more careful about spending his money from this paycheck. However, he wants to buy new sneakers. Keith would use his whole paycheck if he bought the sneakers. He knows he has other **expenses**, or payments he must make. If he buys sneakers, he will not have enough money for his car payment, insurance, and gas.

Computer banking software makes it easy to keep a budget.

Keith needs to set up a **budget** to help him manage his money. A budget is a plan for spending money. A budget is a way to take control of your money.

Maybe you do not have a job. The only money you have might be an allowance. A budget can still help you buy the things you want or need. Sticking to a budget will also keep you from wasting your money. You will not buy things you do not really want or need.

Setting Up a Budget

To begin making a budget, list your expenses for each week or month. Here are Keith's monthly car expenses.

Car payment	$120
Car insurance	100
Gas	60
Total	$280

Keith also sets aside $50 a month for movies, snacks, and other fun things. Keith might spend more or less than $50 on these things each month. Some of your expenses may change every month, too. However, Keith needs to stay on his budget in order to learn how to manage his money. Here are Keith's total expenses for a month.

Car expenses	$280
Entertainment	50
Total	$330

The other part of setting up a budget is figuring out your income. If Keith works 20 hours in a week, he gets a check for $85.30 for that week. In four weeks his income will be four times $85.30, or about $340. However, Keith needs most of his income to pay his expenses. After Keith pays these expenses, he has only $10 left over. See page 214.

```
$340   income from his job
-330   expenses for his car and fun things
$ 10
```

Practice

Keith only has $10 a month left over. Answer these questions on a separate sheet of paper.

1. How many months would Keith have to save to buy sneakers that cost $80?

2. How many months would Keith have to save to buy a new tire for his car that costs $50?

15-5 ▸ Staying on a Budget

Using Technology

Some banks allow customers to transfer money between accounts. You might transfer money into a savings account online for a future purchase.

Keith still wants to buy new sneakers. However, he wants to stay on his budget. So he will have to save for the sneakers. He must make his car payment. If he cannot make payments, the company that sold him the car will take it back.

The law says he must have car insurance. If he does not pay his insurance bill every month, his insurance will be canceled. Then Keith will not be able to drive.

If Keith really wants those sneakers, he might be able to increase his income. He could work more hours at his job on weekends. His grandmother gave him $20 for his birthday. He can add that to his savings.

Keith could also lower his expenses. For example, he could spend less than the $50 in his budget for entertainment and put any money he did not spend toward the sneakers. Keith must remember not to spend more than $50 on fun things. If he spends an extra $5 on pizza, he will have only $5 left over that month to save for the sneakers.

Keith might also be able to save money by spending less on gas. Maybe he could walk places more often or ride with friends. He could also take the bus. If his car needs a new tire or a repair, Keith would have to spend some of the money he has saved to fix his car. Then he will have to wait even longer for his sneakers.

Different Budgets for Different Needs

As Keith knows, having a car is very expensive. He spends most of his paycheck on his car. However, Keith really enjoys having a car. He is willing to spend most of his money on it.

Keith's friend Joy does not have a car. However, she still has to make a budget for her expenses. Joy is saving money from her job for something different. She wants to go to college after she graduates from high school. Joy has set up a budget to help herself reach this goal. She wants different things than Keith does, so her budget is different from his. Here are Joy's monthly expenses.

You can use a calculator to help you balance your budget.

Clothing	$ 60
Entertainment	40
Savings for college	200
Total	$300

Joy's parents earn more than she does. However, they know it is still wise to manage your money, no matter how much you have. Like Joy, they have a budget. Here are their monthly expenses.

Home mortgage payment	$800
Electricity, gas, and water bills	150
Car payment	350
Gasoline	150
Credit card payment	300
Food	350
Entertainment	70
Clothing	120
Total expenses	$2,290

Practice

On a separate sheet of paper, plan a budget for a teenager who earns $400 a month. Then show your budget to a partner. Discuss how your budgets differ. Share your budgets with the class.

15-6 ▸ Planning Ahead

Together, Joy's parents earn about $2,800 a month. After they pay their expenses of $2,290, they have $510 left over. Here is what they do with that $510.

Savings to send Joy to college	$160
Savings for their own retirement	250
Savings for emergencies	100
Total	$510

Joy's parents want to pay for Joy's college. However, they must also plan ahead for their own **retirement.** Retirement is the period after a person stops working and earning income. Many people retire at the age of 65.

Social Security is a government-run retirement savings program. While Joy's parents work, a certain amount of money is taken out of their paychecks for Social Security. After Joy's parents retire and reach the age of at least 62, they will receive a check each month from the United States government. This Social Security check will help them pay some of their expenses.

However, Joy's parents know the Social Security checks will not be enough to pay for all their expenses. That is why they are saving some of their income now for their retirement in the future.

Joy and Keith could start saving for their retirement now, too. It seems far away, but it is best to start saving for retirement as soon as you can.

Joy's parents also set aside money for unexpected expenses or emergencies. Joy and Keith should do that, too. Planning ahead for emergencies and unexpected needs is part of living on your own.

How Budgets Help You

Setting up a budget does not mean you have to save all your money. It does not mean you cannot buy the things you want. Instead, a budget can help you keep track of your money and learn to spend it wisely. That way, your money will not seem to disappear.

Having a budget also makes you think about how you spend money. You may think of more ways to save money. You may also find ways to buy more with whatever money you have. For example, suppose you decide to spend less on movies each month in order to save more money. You might rent a videotape instead of going to a movie theater.

Setting up a budget can help you reach your goals. A budget helps you work toward your goal, step by step.

Money Decisions

Sometimes you have to make difficult decisions about money. Knowing what is important in your life will help you make these decisions.

Think About It

Why is being able to manage your money an important part of living on your own?

Remember
Identify your needs before you choose a job. Money may not be the most important thing.

The way you use money shows what is important to you. For example, you might decide to buy a small gift for a parent instead of something for yourself.

You might even pass up a chance to work for pay. Instead, you might volunteer by donating your time. For example, you might help at an animal shelter or a day care center.

Everyone needs some money. However, do not ever let your need for money tempt you to do things that are harmful or against your beliefs. For example, people who value honesty would not keep money they did not earn. They could not enjoy spending it.

Learning how to make decisions about money is part of preparing to live on your own. Being able to manage your money is a valuable skill. It will help you the rest of your life.

Practice

Suppose you earn $50 per week. On a separate sheet of paper, write a budget for yourself. If you run short of money, how can you fix your budget?

YOU DECIDE
How to Manage Money Wisely

Read the situation below. Then help Keith decide what to do.

Think back to Keith's problem at the beginning of the chapter. He was having trouble managing his money. Keith realized that he had to be more careful about what he spent his money on.

Keith still wants a new pair of sneakers that cost $80. However, he does not want to save $10 a month to buy them. He wants them as soon as possible so he can wear them at track practice.

Right now, business is slow at Grant's Grocery Store. That means Keith cannot work extra hours at the store to make more money. He has to think of other ways to increase his income or lower his expenses.

On a separate sheet of paper, follow the steps below to help Keith make a decision.

STEP 1 Identify the decision Keith must make.

STEP 2 List Keith's choices.

STEP 3 Cross out any choices that are harmful or might be against Keith's beliefs.

STEP 4 Think about the possible results of the remaining choices.

STEP 5 Select the best choice.

STEP 6 Explain how Keith would carry out those choices.

STEP 7 Describe the possible results of Keith's choices.

Make a Difference
What advice would you give Keith about saving up for the new sneakers?

Summary

Businesses pay their employees with paychecks. A paycheck stub shows earnings and deductions.
To cash a check, go to a bank or check-cashing business and prove who you are. A driver's license is a good document to use.
A budget is a spending plan. To set up a budget, list your expenses and income.
Staying on your budget is important. It helps you have enough money to pay your expenses.
People save money for small and large items. They save to meet their goals. People also save for retirement and for emergencies.
Setting up a budget gives you more control over your money. It helps you pay your bills and save for the things you want.

Vocabulary Review

Write *true* or *false*. If a statement is false, change the underlined word or words to make it true. Use a separate sheet of paper.

1. The amount an employee receives after deductions are taken out is <u>gross pay</u>.

2. A form that is attached to a paycheck is a <u>paycheck stub</u>.

3. A plan for spending money is a <u>deduction</u>.

4. The amount of money you earn is your <u>income</u>.

5. A bank employee who works behind the counter is a <u>teller</u>.

6. A government program that takes money out of each employee's paycheck is <u>retirement</u>.

7. When you sign your name on the back of a check, you <u>endorse</u> it.

Chapter Quiz

Write your answers in complete sentences.

1. What kind of information is on a paycheck?

2. What kind of information is shown on a paycheck stub?

3. Where can you go to cash a check?

4. Why do banks ask people for identification before they cash their checks?

5. Do you need to have a full-time job before you set up a budget? Why or why not?

6. What are two things you could do if you wanted to save more money?

7. **CRITICAL THINKING** Why should you start saving for your retirement even if you are very young?

Writing Activity

Some parents require their teens to save a certain part of their income. Do you think this is fair? Should teens be forced to save? Why or why not? Write your ideas in a paragraph on a separate sheet of paper.

Group Activity

Work with a partner to set up a budget for Pam. Pam gets an allowance of $10 every Sunday. However, she usually spends it all by Wednesday. Pam and her friends stop for pizza every day after school. Pam always buys a slice of pizza and a soda. List ways she could have fun with her friends without spending money.

When you shop, think about the things you really need, and find the best prices for them. How can a sale help you choose what to buy?

Learning Objectives

- Explain the difference between a want and a need.
- Describe how setting up a budget can help you be a wise consumer.
- Identify ways that ads try to convince people to buy things.
- List things that make someone a wise consumer.
- Explain what you can do if you are not happy with a product.

Chapter 16 ▷ Being a Wise Consumer

Words to Know

need	something you must have
want	something you would like but can do without
impulse	a sudden act, done without thinking it through
unit pricing	how much a product costs per unit of weight or volume
refund	a return of money
exchange	a trade of one item for another
warranty	a written promise that a product will work for a certain amount of time
service contract	a written promise by a store or company to fix a product if it breaks within a certain time

You might have friends like Bonita and Shakira in the story below. They both have the same amount of money for clothing, but they spend it differently.

When Bonita starts her new job, she looks like a fashion model. She has the newest style of skirts, shirts, and shoes, along with the latest haircut. By the end of the year, Bonita is bored with her clothes. Yet she cannot afford to buy the newer styles she wants.

Shakira has enough clothes to make her happy. She never buys clothes she knows she will tire of easily. No matter where she goes, Shakira has the right thing to wear. She always looks and feels comfortable.

Shakira is a wise consumer. Unlike Bonita, who spends her clothing money quickly, Shakira knows how to make the most of her money. This chapter will help you learn how to become a wise consumer. You will learn when to buy and when not to buy clothes, CDs, sports equipment, or anything else.

16-1 ▶ Understanding Needs and Wants

People buy things for many different reasons. They often tell themselves that they need to buy something. Yet they often just want it and do not really need it. People really need food, water, and protection from the weather. Students often need notebooks, pencils, bus fare, and lunch money.

People want many other things. Some might want in-line skates or a fancy haircut they saw in a magazine. Or they might want the latest jeans or a ticket to a concert. These are not needs. They are wants. A **need** is something you must have. A **want** is something you would like but can do without. Living without a want will not cause any harm.

Think About It

Could a *want* ever become a *need*? Could a *need* ever become a *want*? Explain.

Practice

On a separate sheet of paper, list three things you might need to buy. Then list three things you might want to buy. Compare your lists with a partner. Then discuss these questions.

1. What should a person buy first—the things he or she needs or the things he or she wants? Why?

2. Do you think some people should change the way they spend their money? If so, what changes should they make?

People have other kinds of needs besides physical ones. For example, people who buy a car need to make car payments. People who make long-distance phone calls need to pay their telephone bills. If they do not pay these bills, the companies will take back their cars or disconnect their telephone service.

Steve bought a car he wanted. Now he needs to make his car payments. The car Steve wanted has become a payment he needs to make.

If you buy all the things you want, you may not have enough money for all the things you need. For example, if you spend all your money on the jeans you want, you may not have the bus fare you need to get to school or work. To avoid these problems, you can set up a budget and stick to it.

Think back to Shakira from the beginning of this chapter. In August, Shakira had enough money to buy clothes for the winter. Shakira carefully looked over the clothes she

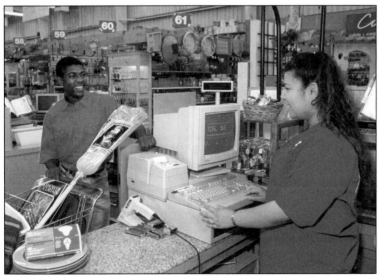

Be sure to buy the things you need before the things you want.

already had. She decided what new clothes she needed. Then she made a budget. By keeping to her budget, she bought the clothes she needed. Her budget kept her from wasting her money on fashions she knew would quickly go out of style. They were too expensive to be in Shakira's budget.

Bonita had the same amount of money for clothes. However, Bonita did not have a budget. She started shopping by looking through fashion magazines. Then she bought the latest styles until her money ran out. It did not take long. The latest fashions were very expensive. Bonita could buy only a few things. Now her friends and family have to hear her say, "I don't have a thing to wear!"

Practice

Suppose you had $100 in your budget to spend on clothes. How would you spend it? Explain your choices on a separate sheet of paper.

Famous people often advertise products.

16-3 ▸ Looking Closely at Ads

Bonita spends money without thinking. She lets herself be influenced by advertisements. Ad writers find many ways to get people to buy things that they may not need. Here are some ways.

1. Some ads try to make you feel that you should buy something because everyone else has it, and you don't want to be left out.

2. Some ads use famous people to sell a product. A movie star or famous model may say a certain shampoo makes her hair shiny. Some people believe what these stars say. However, the stars are actually paid to say these words. The words were written by someone at the shampoo company.

3. Ads for cosmetics or exercise equipment may say a product will make you more attractive than you ever expected to be. However, the models in these ads were probably attractive to begin with. Most people are never going to look like the models in the ads. It does not matter how much skin cream, make-up, or exercise equipment they buy.

4. Many food, drink, and cigarette ads use this message: "Use this product and you will have more fun." They show people having fun together. You are supposed to think they are having fun because they are eating a certain brand of snack or drinking a certain soda. You are not supposed to remember that too many snacks and sodas are not part of a balanced diet or that smoking cigarettes will cause health problems.

▶ **Everyday Tip**
When you see an advertisement, ask yourself whether it is really telling the truth.

5. Some ads try to give you the feeling that the people speaking are your friends and are telling the truth. These ads use ordinary, friendly people, not fashion models. The people smile and tell you they were not sure this product would work. Then they tried it, and it worked. They would not be happy without it. You need it, too. Trust them. This is not necessarily the truth. These words were written by writers, not the people who said them.

6. Ads make it appear that the products will solve any problem someone might have. Most people want to solve their problems, so they buy the product. When you read or hear an advertisement, ask yourself whether it is telling the truth.

Practice

Find three examples of the kinds of ads described on pages 226 and 227. Look in magazines or newspapers. Then show the class what you found. Write whether the ads convince you to buy the products, and why.

16-4 ▶ Becoming a Smart Shopper

When you are thinking of buying something, ask yourself whether you need it. If you do not really need it, check your budget. After you pay for the things you need, decide whether you have enough money left over to buy the item.

After you are sure you need something, gather information about it. If you plan to buy new clothes, check out different brands. Look for brands that are comfortable and attractive. Avoid any brands that might shrink, fade, or fall apart. Choose clothes that you like.

If you ask friends which brands they like, ask why they like them. Do they like a brand because they can wear it for a long time? Do they like it because a favorite movie star wears it? Read newspaper ads. Find out if the item you want is on sale, and compare prices.

Don't let your friends talk you into buying something you really do not need.

Do not let others talk you into buying things you did not plan to buy. Later, you may be sorry you wasted your money.

When you shop, go to several stores and compare prices. Look for sales. If something on your list is on sale, consider buying it. But do not buy something just because it is on sale. You might decide later that you really do not like it. Also, it might not be in your budget. You will be spending money that you need for something else.

Remember, you are not saving money if you never use, wear, or eat what you bought.

Another way to make your money last longer is to shop at less expensive stores. Think about shopping at factory outlets or discount stores. These stores often sell designer clothing at lower prices. Sometimes, this clothing is not perfect. But the problem may be something no one will notice or that you can fix. Check a product carefully before you buy it.

Shopping at a Supermarket

With so many different items to choose from, a supermarket can be a confusing place. Make a list of what you need and stick to it. Avoid **impulse** buying. An impulse is a sudden act that is done without thinking it through. Supermarkets often put magazines and snacks beside the checkout lines. While people wait, they see these things and buy them on impulse. To avoid wasting money, remember your budget. If you buy things on impulse, you may not be able to buy things you really need.

▶ **Everyday Tip**
Try not to shop for food when you are hungry. All of the food will look good. Then you will want to buy things you do not need or want.

Another way of shopping wisely is to check the **unit pricing** on different items. Unit pricing is how much a product costs per unit of volume or weight. A unit could be an ounce, a pound, a serving, or a single item.

For example, one cereal might cost $.34 an ounce while another brand of the same cereal might cost $.47 per ounce. Unit pricing lets you compare brands to see which costs less. You can also compare small and large packages of the same brand to see which is a better buy. You will find a product's unit pricing on a small sign on the store shelf where the product is displayed.

Think About It

Why do some people prefer to buy name brands rather than a store's own brands of food?

Stores often sell their own brands of things. Buying store brands can usually save you money. They are cheaper than the name brands. Some are just as good as other brands.

Try looking for "quick-sale" items. Many stores mark down meat or bread that must be sold quickly or be thrown away. Often you can save money by buying these items. Still, you must eat or freeze them right away. If you keep them without freezing them, they will spoil or get stale.

Buy food in large packages, which usually cost less than smaller ones. But check the unit price first to make sure it is cheaper. As soon as you get home, divide the food into meal-sized portions. Then freeze it right away.

Practice

Suppose one box of cereal weighs 24 ounces and costs $3.60. A smaller box of the same cereal weighs 16 ounces but is on sale for $2.24. On a separate sheet of paper, figure out which box costs less per ounce.

When you want something, you do not always have to buy it. Borrowing from friends and family is one way to avoid spending.

For instance, if you buy a suit or a dress for a special occasion, you might wear it only once. Then it will just hang in your closet. Instead, consider borrowing something to wear from a friend. However, remember to be responsible and have the clothing cleaned before you return it. Do not forget to return it on time.

Trading is another way to save your money. Suppose you need to type a report you just wrote and you do not have a computer. However, your friend has a computer. Your friend might let you use the computer if, in return, you wash your friend's car.

Another way to save money is to shop at secondhand stores and garage sales. Slightly used things can be good bargains. You might find a sweater or even a computer at a very low price.

When Something Goes Wrong

You may buy a product such as a pair of shoes or a hair dryer that you are not happy with when you get home. The shoes might be too small or the hair dryer might not work. You do not always have to keep these things.

You can usually take an item back to the store and get a **refund**, which is a return of money. Or you can ask for an **exchange**, which is a trade of one item for another. That way, you can get shoes that fit or a hair dryer that works.

If a hair dryer does not work, you might want to try another dryer of the same kind. Then you would ask for an exchange. However, if a shirt changed colors in the wash, others like it would probably do the same thing. In that case, you should ask for a refund. Then you can buy a different kind of shirt, maybe at a different store.

Did You Know?

Stores are required by law to explain their return policy to customers. Always ask for this when you make a big purchase.

You can usually return an item for a refund, unless the store's policy is for exchange or credit only.

When you return something to the store, be polite. Remember that the store probably did not mean to sell you something that does not work. Calmly explain why you do not want to keep the product. Then ask for a refund or an exchange. Be firm, but polite.

Successful Returns

Two ways to increase your chances of getting a refund are to save your sales slips and to know the return policy. A sales slip proves you bought the item from that store. It shows when you bought it and how much you paid. If you do not have the sales slip, some stores will not give you a refund or exchange for what you bought.

Other stores may give you credit toward another purchase. This means you cannot get your money back. You can get something else in the store that costs the same. You only get credit for what you paid.

Most stores insist that you have a sales slip to return an item. Some stores will allow you to return items only for a certain amount of time after you buy them. Other stores might not allow any returns. You have to be sure you want the item before you buy it.

There is another good reason to save your sales slips. You can use them to keep track of how you have spent your money. Receipts and sales slips help you when you are making your budget.

Practice

Talk with a partner about what happened when either of you tried to return things to stores. Were you happy about how the store treated you? What could you do differently the next time? Write your experiences on a separate sheet of paper.

16-6 Reading Warranties and Service Contracts

Suppose you used a hair dryer for a month and then it stopped working. In this case, a **warranty** might help. A warranty is a written promise that the product will work for a certain amount of time. Some warranties are for a year.

Many products that have motors also have warranties. The warranty might be printed on the box or on a paper inside the box. Sometimes you might have to

Using Technology

You can find information on extended warranties, new products, and the location of service centers, on a company's Web site.

IN-LINE SKATES LIMITED WARRANTY

Completion of the warranty registration form gives you valuable rights. If you, the purchaser, complete your attached registration form and mail the original to IN-Line Skates, Inc., P.O. Box 082349, Somewhere, NJ 12345 within 10 days of your purchase or receipt of the skates as a gift, your IN-Line skates will be covered by the Limited Warranty described here. Limited Warranty: Subject to registration, your new IN-Line Skates are warranted by an IN-Line dealer within six months of the purchase of your skates from the company. Skates furnished as replacements will continue to be covered under the Limited Warranty until six months from the date of the original purchase.

This is a limited warranty for In-Line skates.

fill out a card and mail it to the manufacturer to get a warranty on what you bought.

The warranty will explain what to do if the product stops working. You might have to take it back to the store or mail it to the manufacturer. Before you buy an expensive product, read its warranty carefully. It might cover only part of the cost of repairing the product. It might be wiser to buy something with a better warranty.

You might also buy something that would cost a lot to repair, such as a stereo or an air conditioner. Then the store may offer to sell you a service contract. A **service contract** promises to fix a product if it breaks within a certain time. One service contract may promise to fix the product for free if it stops working within a year. Another service contract might warranty a product for two or three years. Some contracts promise to replace parts that break, but you must pay the cost of the labor.

Think carefully before you buy a service contract. It might cost more than the actual repairs. If you do not need repairs during the time of the contract, you cannot get your money back.

Consuming Wisely

Being a wise consumer means buying what you need first. Then you can use any extra money to buy what you want. It also means remembering that ads are designed to get people to buy products. They are not written to explain anything bad about a product.

The tips in this chapter should help you make the most of your money. Learning to spend money wisely is one more way to get ready to live on your own.

Practice

Write a letter to a friend explaining the difference between a warranty and a service contract. Tell your friend when it is better to buy a service contract.

Read the situation below. Then help Anthony decide what to do.

Anthony and Kurt are at the mall. Anthony has found a pair of jeans he really likes that costs $45. Anthony has $50 in his budget for new jeans. However, Kurt wants Anthony to buy a different pair. Kurt likes the designer pair he saw someone wear in a movie. The designer jeans are on sale today for only $35.

On a separate sheet of paper, follow the steps below to help Anthony decide which pair to buy.

STEP 1   Identify the decision Anthony must make.

STEP 2   List Anthony's choices.

STEP 3   Cross out any choices that are harmful or might be against Anthony's beliefs. For example, telling Kurt to mind his own business would be rude.

STEP 4   Think about the possible results of the remaining choices.

STEP 5   Select the best choice.

STEP 6   Explain how Anthony would carry out this choice.

STEP 7   Describe the possible results of Anthony's choice.

Make a Difference

What advice would you give Anthony if a friend tells him to buy something different from his own choice?

Summary

A need is something you must have, like food. A want is something you would like to have but could do without, like new jeans.
Ads try to convince people to buy things. Before you read ads, decide what you want and what you really need to buy.
Make sure you need or can afford what you plan to buy. Gather information so you know which brand to buy and where it is on sale. Do not let other people influence you to buy something you do not want or need.
When you shop, compare prices at several stores. Buy things based on what is important to you, such as style, cost, or fit. Be wise about buying on sale.
Avoid impulse buying. Before you go to the supermarket, make a list of what you need. Be sure to check the unit pricing of items.
Before you buy anything, find out the store's return policy. Save your sales slips to make returning things easier.
Read product warranties and service contracts carefully. Service contracts may cost more than they are worth.

Vocabulary Review

service contract

want

unit pricing

exchange

warranty

impulse

need

refund

Write a term from the list that matches each definition below.

1. a return of money

2. a sudden act

3. something you would like but can do without

4. a written promise that a product will work for a certain amount of time

5. a trade of one item for another

6. something you must have

7. the price per unit of weight or volume

8. a written promise by a store or company to fix a product if it breaks within a certain time

Chapter Quiz

Write your answers in complete sentences.

1. What are two examples of a need and two examples of a want?

2. What should you buy first—things that you need or things that you want? Why?

3. When should you buy something that is on sale?

4. What is the difference between a refund and an exchange?

5. Why is it important to save sales slips?

6. If a store offers you a service contract, should you buy it? Why or why not?

7. **CRITICAL THINKING** How can taking a list to the grocery store help you save money?

Writing Activity

The United States government has laws called "truth in advertising." That means companies are not allowed to say things about their products that are not true. Find an ad that you think goes against these laws. Write a paragraph explaining what the ad says. Tell why you think the ad does not tell the truth about the product.

Group Activity

You want to buy a new bike. Talk with a partner about four features you are looking for and four things you would do before buying the bike. Together, make a checklist of these items. Make copies of the checklist to share with the class. Compare your ideas.

Sometimes credit cards make it too easy to buy things. How can credit cards cause you problems?

Learning Objectives

- Explain why it is important to pay bills on time.
- Describe how credit cards work.
- Explain what minimum payment and interest mean in relation to credit cards.
- Describe the good and bad points of using credit cards.
- Explain a credit report.
- Describe how to get and keep a good credit report.

Chapter 17 — Using Credit Wisely

Words to Know

consumer	someone who buys things
bill	a written request for money for something you bought
due date	the date by which a bill should be paid
late fee	an extra charge when a bill is not paid on time
credit	money that you borrow from a bank, store, or credit card company to pay for things you buy
loan	money borrowed from a bank and paid back in regular payments
interest	a fee you pay to borrow money or a payment you receive when you keep your money in a bank account
credit card	a card that lets you buy something now but pay for it later
minimum payment	the smallest payment that will be accepted
credit report	a report of whether you have paid your bills or loans on time
credit bureau	a business that puts together credit reports
cosigner	a person who agrees to pay for someone else's credit card bill if that person cannot pay it

Read the situation. Find out what happened to Andy when he did not pay a bill.

> Andy ordered a CD from a CD club. When the bill for $17.50 came, he did not pay it. When Andy got another bill from the CD club, he still owed $17.50 for the CD, plus an extra $5 because he had not paid his first bill.

Everyone is a **consumer**, or someone who buys things. After people buy things, they receive bills. A **bill** is a written request for money for something you bought. Paying people what you owe them is part of being responsible. It is an important part of living on your own. You may not receive many bills right now, but as time goes by, you will. Now is a good time for you to start learning good bill-paying habits.

17-1 ▶ Being Responsible About Paying Bills

Paying bills on time helps make you a responsible consumer. Nearly every bill you receive will have a **due date** on it. The company expects you to pay the bill by this date. If your payment is late, the company may add a **late fee** to your bill. A late fee is an extra charge for not sending your payment in on time. The company may add a late fee if you do not send a payment at all.

You may be charged a late fee for certain kinds of payments. These include payments for rent, telephone service, electricity, gas, and water. Many credit card companies also charge large late fees, often $25 or more.

Usually, a company will not call and remind you to pay a bill the first month it is late. A late fee will just appear on your next bill. This is what happened to Andy.

Late Payments
If your payment is very late, you might have to pay more than a late fee. For example, the electric company might shut off your electricity if you do not pay your electric bill. Then you would have to pay a

fee to have it turned back on. This fee would be higher than a late fee. If you had to pay this fee more than one time, this could get very expensive.

It is much cheaper and more responsible to pay your bills on time. When you receive a bill, check to see when it is due. Then pay the bill by that date. That way, you will never have to worry about late fees.

Did You Know ?

Most bills include a customer service phone number. If you think there is a mistake on your bill, or you cannot tell when a bill is due, call customer service.

Practice

Think of ways that Andy could have avoided being charged the late fee. Write your ideas on a separate sheet of paper. Then share your ideas with the class.

17-2 ▸ Understanding Credit

Some people buy things on **credit.** Credit is money that you borrow from a bank, store, or credit card company to pay for things you buy. You repay the money later.

A **loan** is one kind of credit. It is money borrowed from the bank to buy something expensive, such as a car. You pay it back on a schedule. You also pay the bank **interest**, a charge for borrowing money.

Another way to use credit is to have a **credit card**, a card that lets you buy something now but pay for it later. You can get a credit card from a bank or credit card company. Some department stores and gasoline companies also offer credit cards. If you have a credit card, you can buy things without using cash or checks.

When you use a credit card, you are borrowing money from the credit card company. You are using that money to buy something from a store. The credit card company pays the store for what you bought. Then you pay the credit card company for what you bought.

When you use a credit card, you sign a slip of paper. Your signature is a promise to pay your credit card bill when it comes in the mail.

Buying With a Credit Card

It is easy to buy things with a credit card. You do not need to have cash with you. You can get what you want right away. However, using a credit card can lead to problems.

Andy recently got a credit card in the mail. Andy used his new credit card to buy a pair of jeans. He had wanted the jeans for a month, and now he could finally get them. A few weeks later, Andy got a bill from the credit card company for $70.

▶ **Everyday Tip**
Always try to pay more than the minimum payment. If you do, you will not have to pay as much interest to the credit card company.

However, the bill said the **minimum payment** was only $10. Andy knew that a minimum payment was the smallest payment the credit card company would accept. That meant he could pay only $10 this month. He thought he could pay the other $60 later.

Andy had not set aside money in his budget to pay for the jeans. However, he did have $10 for the minimum payment. Andy decided to send the company a check for $10.

The next month, the credit card company sent Andy a second bill. It was for $60.90. The extra $.90 was for interest. (See Andy's bill on the next page.) This kind of interest, or finance charge, is money you pay to a credit card company when you borrow money. It is different from the interest a bank pays to you when you have a savings or checking account.

SIB CREDIT COMPANY	PLEASE INDICATE NAME, ADDRESS, OR TELEPHONE CHANGES HERE				

A SIB Credit Company

HOME (   )

WORK (   )

SIB 06 17 88
54321   1234

Account Number	Payment Due Date	New Balance	Past Due Amount	Minimum Payment	Please write in amount of enclosed payment
23-45-789	09/13/01	$60.90	$0.00	$10.00	$

USE ENCLOSED ENVELOPE
AND MAKE PAYMENTS TO:

PLEASE DETACH TOP PORTION AND ENCLOSE WITH PAYMENT

▼

SIB Investments
P.O. Box 061788
Camden, NJ 08104-4321

||||||||||||||||||||||||||||||||||||||||

Andy Davis
12 East Broadway Street
Galloway, IL 54321-1234

This is a credit card bill.

The minimum payment on the second bill was still $10, so Andy paid that. Andy thought his next bill would be for $50.90. But it was for $51.66. The credit card company was adding more interest every month. Andy began to think he would never be able to pay for those jeans.

Andy was still borrowing money from the credit card company. As long as Andy owed the credit card company money, he would have to pay interest on the amount he owed.

You can avoid paying any interest on a credit card. You just have to pay the entire amount you owe when you get the bill every month. Then the credit card company will not charge you interest.

Practice

Look at the credit card bill on this page. Then answer these three questions on a separate sheet of paper:

1. When is Andy's next payment due?

2. What is the least amount of money Andy can pay on this bill?

3. What is the full amount of the bill?

Credit card companies are in business to make money. They do this by charging three main fees.

1. The first is an *annual fee*. This is a fee you pay the credit card company every year to use its card. This fee might be $20 or more. Not all credit card companies charge an annual fee. You can save money if you find out which companies do not charge an annual fee. Credit cards from department stores and gasoline companies often do not charge an annual fee.

2. Credit card companies make most of their money by charging *interest*. The companies hope you will not pay your entire bill every month. If you pay the whole amount, they cannot get any extra money from you. However, many people just make the minimum payment. Then the credit card company charges them interest on the rest of their bill.

   Remember, interest is another way credit card companies make money. Different cards charge different amounts of interest. Interest can be as low as 5.9 percent or higher than 18 percent. You can save money by looking for a credit card with a low interest rate.

3. Many credit card companies also charge *late fees*. A late fee can be higher than a minimum payment. Suppose Andy had no money when he received the $70 bill for his jeans. He could not even make the minimum payment of $10.

Think About It

Which is a less expensive way to pay, with cash or a credit card? Why?

The next month Andy would receive another bill from the credit card company. Now he would have to pay interest on the $70 he owed. For Andy's card, that would be about $1.05. Then the credit card company might add a late fee of $15. Now Andy would owe $86.05. (See Andy's notebook on the next page.)

for the jeans	$70.00
for interest on the $70	1.05
for a late fee	15.00
	$86.05

When you are choosing a credit card, try to avoid cards with an annual fee. If you do not pay your total bill each month, look for a card with a low interest rate.

Problems with "Plastic"

A slang term for *credit cards* is "plastic" because that is what the cards are made of. Some people buy too many things with their plastic. They do not plan how they will pay for the things they buy on credit.

Some people use several credit cards. Every month, they get bills from several credit card companies. These bills are often more than they can pay. So these people make only the minimum payment on each bill. Then they must pay interest on the money they still owe.

People can develop huge credit card bills. Companies will usually cancel credit cards if people cannot make the minimum payments. You can avoid these problems if you learn how to manage your money.

Credit Card Advantages

There are many advantages to having a credit card. You do not have to carry a lot of cash with you. You can also buy things through the mail or by phone. Credit cards can be useful in an emergency. If you do not have the money with you and you need something badly, you can use your "plastic."

Did You Know ?

As many as half of the households in America have trouble making their minimum credit card payments.

Practice

Think of three reasons why someone your age should or should not get a credit card. Write them on a separate sheet of paper.

17-4 ▶ Applying for a Credit Card

If you want a credit card, you usually have to apply for one. That means you will have to ask a bank or credit card company to give you one. To do this, you will have to fill out an application form.

Most credit card applications ask for your name, address, phone number, Social Security number, and birthdate. They also want to know where you work and how long you have worked there. The companies will want to know how much you earn each month or each year. They may also ask for your checking or savings account numbers and whether you have any other credit cards.

The credit card company will check the information you put on your application. They might call your bank and your employer to make sure what you wrote down was correct. The credit card company wants to make sure that you earn enough money to pay your credit card bill.

If the company gives you a card, it may set a limit on how much you can charge on the card. The less income you have, the less you will be able to charge. The more income you have, the more you will be able to charge.

Practice

Get a credit card application and fill it out. Ask a teacher or family member to help you find one. You can work with a partner.

17-5 ▶ Understanding Credit Reports

To find out whether you pay your bills on time, the credit card company will check your **credit report**. A credit report tells whether you have paid your other bills or loans on time. Each time you are late on a payment or have a credit card canceled, that information is added to your credit report.

A business called a **credit bureau** collects the information about how people pay their bills. The credit bureau puts together a credit report on each person. A credit card company can get your credit report from the credit bureau. You can also request a copy of your credit report from the credit bureau.

If you are applying for your first credit card, there is probably no credit report for you. In this case, the credit card company may ask you to have a **cosigner.** A cosigner is usually a family member who already has a good credit report. You and your cosigner both sign your credit card application. This means that your cosigner agrees to pay your credit card bill if you cannot pay it.

Using Technology

You can request your credit report on the Internet. Two credit bureaus are www.equifax.com and www.tuc.com.

How to Get a Good Credit Report

Over time, you can get a good credit report. But you have to start somewhere. To start to build a good credit report, apply for a credit card from a local store. If you need a cosigner, get one. Then buy some items with your new credit card. When your bill arrives, pay the whole amount. This will be reported to the credit bureau. After a period of time your credit report will show that you are a responsible person.

To keep your good credit report, you must continue to pay your bills on time. At some point, you will probably want to get a loan to buy a car. If you have paid your bills on time, a bank will be much more willing to give you a loan. They will know you are a responsible person.

People who miss credit card and loan payments or pay bills late have bad credit reports. Banks and credit card companies read these reports. They often turn these people down when they ask for a loan or credit card.

Practice

On a separate sheet of paper, list two ways you would get a good credit report and two ways you would get a bad credit report.

17-6 ▶ Protecting Your Credit Card

If your credit card is lost or stolen, other people might buy things with it. You need to protect your credit card. Write down the card number and the name of the credit card company for each of your cards. Keep this information in a safe place.

If your card gets lost or stolen, call the credit card company right away. Then someone else will not be able to charge things on your card. If someone has already used your card, you will not have to pay for those charges.

Save your credit card receipts. When you get your monthly bill, make sure only the things you bought are listed. If you see a mistake, call the company.

Do not give your credit card number to anyone on the telephone, unless you have called a company yourself. You do not know for sure who is calling you. Never lend your credit card to anyone.

Finally, if you get a new credit card, cut up the old one and throw it away. Then no one else can use it.

Practice

With a partner, list three situations in which you would need to call a credit card company. Then role-play the situations you listed.

Read the situation below. Then help Andy decide what to do.

Andy wants to buy a set of weights so he can work out at home. He found one set that costs $200. He only has $103 now. He makes $50 a week at his part-time job. Andy wants the weights right away, so he is thinking about buying them with his credit card.

On a separate sheet of paper, follow the steps below. Help Andy decide the best way to pay for the weights.

STEP 1 Identify the problem Andy must solve.

STEP 2 List Andy's choices.

STEP 3 Cross out any choices that are harmful or might be against Andy's beliefs.

STEP 4 Think about the possible results of the remaining choices.

STEP 5 Select the best choice.

STEP 6 Explain how Andy would carry out this choice.

STEP 7 Describe the possible results of Andy's choice.

Make a Difference

How do you think Andy should pay for the weights? Why?

Summary

People who pay their bills late are often charged a fee.
When you use a credit card, you are borrowing money from a credit card company. The company charges you interest.
You can make a minimum payment on a credit card bill. However, you will then have to pay interest on what you still owe.
Some people buy too many things with their credit cards. Then they are unable to pay their credit card bills.
Credit cards can be helpful if you use them wisely. You do not have to carry lots of cash all the time.
You fill out an application to get most credit cards. The credit card company decides whether you can afford to make payments.
A credit report tells whether you have paid your bills on time.
Protect your cards to prevent others from using them.

Vocabulary Review

consumer
bill
due date
late fee
loan
minimum payment
credit bureau

Complete each sentence with a term from the list. Use a separate sheet of paper.

1. The smallest payment that will be accepted is a ——.

2. A written request for money for something you bought is a ——.

3. Someone who buys things is a ——.

4. A business that puts together credit reports is a ——.

5. An extra charge when a bill is not paid on time is a ——.

6. Money that is borrowed and is paid back in regular payments is a ——.

7. The date by which a bill should be paid is its ——.

Chapter Quiz

Write your answers in complete sentences.

1. What can happen if you pay your bills late?

2. When you sign a credit card slip, what are you promising to do?

3. Winona received a large credit card bill. She cannot pay all of it. Should she make a minimum payment, or should she ignore the bill? Why?

4. What can happen to people who have a bad credit report?

5. What are two ways that credit cards are helpful?

6. What are two ways you can protect your credit card?

7. **CRITICAL THINKING** Why do some people have a problem with their credit cards?

Writing Activity

It is easy to buy things with credit cards. Some people spend more than they should. Some people believe that young people tend to spend more money because they have less experience managing money. Do you think that a person under the age of 21 should be allowed to have a credit card? Write your opinions in a paragraph on a separate sheet of paper.

Group Activity

Work with a group to make up five rules for paying bills and using credit cards. Write them on poster board. Discuss your rules with the class. Display the poster in your classroom.

Unit 5 **Review**

Read each sentence below. Then choose the letter that best completes each one.

1. All of the following are charged by a bank, except
   A. check fees.
   B. deposit fees.
   C. service charges.
   D. ATM fees.

2. All of the following are shown on a paycheck stub except
   A. how much an employee earned.
   B. how much tax was taken out.
   C. how well the employee does his or her job.
   D. how many hours the employee worked.

3. A smart supermarket shopper
   A. compares brands and prices.
   B. checks unit pricing.
   C. makes a list and sticks to it.
   D. all of the above

4. People who pay their bills late
   A. are given more credit.
   B. are often charged late fees.
   C. are forgiven if they say they are sorry.
   D. are encouraged to use their card more.

5. When you write a check, you should not
   A. use a pen.
   B. write the date.
   C. sign a blank check.
   D. write the amount in numbers and words.

6. A budget helps you to
   A. spend any way you wish.
   B. avoid saving for the future.
   C. decide where your money is going.
   D. all of the above

7. A credit card bill does not show you
   A. the color of the items you bought.
   B. what your balance is.
   C. when the payment is due.
   D. what the minimum payment is.

Critical Thinking

Jamal is thinking about buying a leather coat that costs nearly $300. He does not know whether he can afford it. How could setting up a budget help him?

WRITING Suppose you buy something and decide later that you do not like it. What are some things you can do about it? Write a short essay to explain your answer.

Unit 6 ▷ Living on Your Own

Getting from one place to another can be easy, if you know how. What types of transportation are available in your community?

Learning Objectives

- Identify reasons not to buy a car.
- Describe the benefits of using public transportation.
- Explain how to read a bus schedule.
- Explain how to choose a car.
- Describe the costs of owning a car.
- Explain how to get a driver's license.
- Describe a responsible driver.

Chapter 18 ▶ Getting Places

Words to Know

public transportation	a system of buses, trains, and subways that is available to everyone for a small fee
car pools	groups of people who share rides in each other's cars
route	a certain path or direction
temporary learner's permit	permission to practice driving with a licensed driver in the car
mechanic	a person who repairs car engines
service	to take care of a car's needs, such as changing the oil and adjusting the engine
down payment	the first payment on a large purchase such as a car
car insurance	money you pay a company each month so that the company will pay for repairs after an accident

Living on your own can be difficult. Read the story below to find out what is worrying Greg.

Greg was reading the newspaper "Want Ads" for an hour. He was looking for a job. He saw jobs that interested him. Greg's problem was that he could not get to many of them.

"If I had a car, I could drive anywhere," he told himself. "Then I could apply for more jobs." Greg could not afford to buy a car because he did not have a job. However, he could not get a job unless he could find a way to get there.

One of the challenges of living on your own is getting where you need to go. If you do not have a car, this might seem difficult. However, you do not always need to have a car to get around. This chapter will help you explore other ways to go from one place to another. You will also learn how to get a driver's license and a car—if that is what you want.

18-1 ▶ Understanding Public Transportation

Many people do not have cars for many reasons. Some people want a car but cannot afford one. Other people choose not to get a car. Cars are expensive to buy. Cars also cost a lot after you buy them. You must pay for insurance, gas, and repairs. There are other costs as well.

In large cities, people may not have any place to park a car. They often have to pay to park their cars in a parking lot.

Most cities have **public transportation.** Public transportation is a system of buses, trains, and subways that is available to everyone for a small fee. Tax money helps pay for these buses, trains, and subways. This keeps the cost for riders low.

Millions of people use public transportation every day. They go to work, school, stores, and friends' homes. In fact, they go almost every place a car would take them within the city.

Finding Public Transportation

You can use the phone book to find out whether your community has public transportation services. Look in the government pages of your local phone book. You can find the telephone number for your town or city and call the general number. Then you can ask what public transportation is available. Only the largest cities, such as New York City, Boston, and Washington, DC, have subways or commuter trains. Small towns

Using Technology

Many public transportation companies list their schedules and fares on the Internet. You can quickly find out when transportation is available and how much it will cost.

may not even have their own bus service. However, many cities do have some type of public transportation to help you get around.

If your town does not have its own buses, maybe buses from a nearby city pass through your town each day. Or maybe your town has set up **car pools.** Car pools are groups of people who share rides in each other's cars. You can sometimes get information on car pools by calling your local government office.

Practice

Find out what public transportation is available in your town or city. Write down what you learn about getting around in your community.

18-2 ▸ Reading a Bus Schedule

Before you can use a bus, you have to know where to find one and where it is going. Begin by getting a bus schedule. A bus schedule explains when and where the buses go. Your library might have copies of local bus schedules.

You can also call bus companies and ask how to get a bus schedule. Look in the Yellow Pages in the telephone book. Look under "Bus" for the telephone numbers of different bus companies. If you know the name of the bus company, look in the white business pages of the telephone book. Look under the name of the bus company for the telephone number. Do not forget, you can also use a computer to find this information.

Bus schedules look different in different cities. However, they all show the **route** the buses travel through the city. A route is a certain path or direction.

▶ **Everyday Tip**
Keep a bus schedule with you at all times. Then if you need an earlier bus, you will know when one comes.

Look at the bus route map below. The dark line is the path the bus follows. Streets that the bus route crosses are shown so you can find where to get on and off the bus.

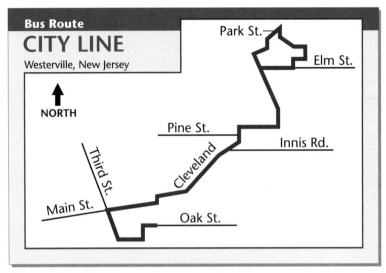

Bus route map

Information about when buses arrive is found on the back of the bus route map. It shows that two buses follow the same route. Below is part of the schedule for Bus A and Bus B.

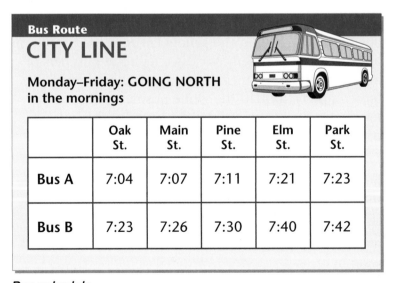

Bus schedule

Practice

Use the bus route map and bus schedule on page 258 to answer these questions.

1. If you wanted to go to Innis Road, at which stop would you get off?

2. If you had to be at Elm Street by 7:30, would you take Bus A or Bus B?

3. If you got on Bus A at Oak Street, how long would it take you to get to Elm Street?

18-3 ▶ Getting a Driver's License

If you want to drive a car, you need a driver's license. A driver's license allows you to drive a car legally. It also proves who you are. It is a form of identification, or ID. A driver's license with your name, picture, and signature can also help you cash a check or use a credit card.

To get a driver's license in many states, you must be at least 16 years old and pass two tests. One is a written test, and the other is a driving test.

Begin by getting a copy of the booklet that explains your state's traffic laws and signs. You might get this booklet at a driver's license examination center or a highway patrol post. These places may be listed in the government pages of the telephone book or on the Internet. Find the listing for your state and look under "Public Safety Department," "Department of Motor Vehicles," "Highway Patrol," or similar words. Call to ask if they have the booklets.

▶ **Everyday Tip**
Be sure to study the driver's booklet to learn about driving laws and road signs.

You can study the driver's booklet at home to learn the driving laws and signs. You can study for as long as you want. Then you can go to the driver's license examination center. There you will fill out an application for a driver's license.

A temporary learner's permit allows you to practice driving.

The application asks for lots of information about you. Before you go to take the driver's test, call to find out what you need to bring. You will probably need your birth certificate or Social Security card. You may also need other forms of ID. If you are under 18, a parent or guardian may also have to sign your application.

Someone at the exam center will test your eyesight. If you wear glasses or contact lenses, make sure you wear them for the test. You need to prove you can see well enough to drive.

Next, it is time for you to take the written test on driving laws and traffic signs. If you pass, you will receive a **temporary learner's permit.** This allows you to practice driving for six months. However, while you practice, a licensed driver must sit beside you in the car. If you do not pass the written test, you can take it again.

When you are ready to take the driving test, you must make an appointment at the examination station. During the test, an examiner will sit beside you as you drive. The examiner will tell you what route to travel. You must prove you can drive safely and obey the traffic laws. The driver's booklet explains what you need to know for your test.

If you pass the driving test, you will get your license. Do not be discouraged if you fail the test the first time. Many people try several times before they pass the driving test.

Practice

Talk with a friend or family member who has taken the written driver's test. Ask which parts of the test the person thought were difficult. What does this person think would help someone pass the test? Share what you learn with the class.

18-4 ▸ Getting Your Own Car

Cars mean freedom for many young people. They can go where and when they want without asking for a ride. But cars cost a lot of money. Cars are also a big responsibility. Before you decide to get a car, decide whether you really need a car or just want one. Look into other ways to go from place to place.

If you are sure you need a car, you have to decide between a new car and a used one. Almost everyone dreams of buying a brand-new car. A new car comes with a warranty. For example, the warranty might say that the dealer will fix any part that breaks during the first year or the first 12,000 miles.

You can also buy a used car. A used car costs less than a new car. That means you do not have to save as long to get it. Some used cars come with a limited warranty. This would cover some repairs for the first few months that you own the car.

You take a chance when you buy a used car. You often cannot tell whether there are hidden problems in the engine. Cars last only so long. The one you buy might be near the end of its life.

Did You Know ?

Used car dealers buy their cars from previous owners and car companies. They also buy cars from rental agencies, taxi companies, and police departments.

If you are considering buying a used car, have a **mechanic** check it over. A mechanic is a person who works on car engines. You can take a mechanic with you the first time you look at the car, or you can take the car to a car repair shop. Having a mechanic check the car may cost $25 to $50, but it is worth it. It will give you a better idea of what you are buying. A mechanic will know what to check in a car engine. If there is a problem, he or she will be able to find it. You do not want to buy a car that will cost a lot in repairs.

Choosing a Car Model and a Car Dealer

You might have already chosen the model of car you want. Even so, look through magazines that compare cars, such as *Consumer Reports*. There are also magazines that put out guides to used cars. Find out what experts think of the car you have in mind. Another car might have features that you want, but it might cost less and be safer to drive.

If you are buying a new car, visit car dealers that sell the car you want. You need to choose a car dealer by its reputation as well as its prices. Ask friends, neighbors, and family members which car dealers have treated them fairly.

Find out what kind of service the car dealers provide after you buy a car. New car dealers should be happy to fix anything that does not work correctly. Used car dealers may not have service departments.

Be sure to think about a car dealer's location. If you buy a new car, the warranty might require you to have the dealer **service** it. To service a car, the dealer changes the oil, adjusts the engine, and fixes other problems.

You should service or take the car to be serviced every 3,000 to 5,000 miles. If the dealer is far away, that can be a problem. If something is wrong with the car, you will need to take it back to the dealer. It may be easier if the dealer you choose is nearby.

Using Technology

Several sites on the Internet rate new and used cars by providing research and reviews. One of these sites is www.kbb.com.

Paying for a Car

Most people get loans to buy a car. That means they borrow money and have to pay it back over time. Most loans come from banks, but some car dealers can arrange loans for their customers.

You have to apply for a loan. That means you might not get it. If you have a good credit report, you have a better chance of getting a loan. A good credit report means you have been paying your bills on time.

To pay for a new or used car, you will probably make a **down payment**. This is the first payment you make when you buy a car. It will be about 20 percent of the total cost of the car. If a car costs $12,000, the down payment might be $2,400.

You may need to borrow money to cover the rest of the cost. To repay this loan, you will make monthly payments for three or four years, sometimes more. You do not own the car until you have made all of the loan payments.

Your monthly payments will include interest on whatever money you still owe. Suppose you bought a new car for $12,000 and made a down payment of $2,400. Then you would get a loan for the remaining $9,600 for three years.

The bank will figure out how much interest you will have to pay over the three years. They will add that amount to your loan of $9,600. So the actual amount you pay for the car will be more than $9,600. The bank will divide the total amount by 36, which is the number of months in three years. That will be the amount of money you will have to pay the bank each month.

If you repay the loan over a four-year period, you will pay more in interest. Your monthly payments will be less, but you will pay more since you are borrowing money for a longer period.

A down payment is not always needed. If you do not make one, you will pay the whole cost of the car in monthly payments. That will make the payments higher.

Practice

Answer the questions below. Then share your answers with the class.

1. How should you look for a used car?

2. Why is it better to make a large down payment on a car?

18-5 ▸ Getting a Loan

After you choose a car, the dealer will give you a paper showing how much the car costs. You can take that paper to the bank and ask for a loan. The bank will decide whether to lend you money for the car.

Applying for a loan is like applying for a credit card. You will need to fill out forms explaining where you work and how much you earn. The bank wants to make sure you can pay back any money you borrow. You might have to ask a relative or a good friend with a job to cosign your application. The cosigner promises to make your car payments if you cannot.

Remember
Interest is what you pay the bank for lending you money. Some banks have better interest rates and loan terms than others.

If the bank gives you a loan, it will pay the dealer for your car. The bank now owns your car. If you miss a number of payments, the bank can take your car.

If you do not make your payments on time, the bank may charge you a late fee. A late fee could be 10 percent to 20 percent of your payment for the month. If your monthly payment was supposed to be $200, it could increase to $220 or $240. If you are often late in paying, your credit report will show this. The next time you ask for a loan or a credit card, you might not get it.

Car Insurance

What would happen if another driver ran into your car? Your car might be badly damaged. Someone must pay for the repairs on your car. Repairs can be very expensive. That is why most states require all drivers to have **car insurance.** Car insurance is money you pay a company each month so the company will pay for repairs after an accident.

You can get insurance to repair your car even if an accident is your fault and does not involve another car. Most states do not require this kind of insurance. However, if you get a loan, the bank might require you to have this insurance. Remember, the bank owns the car until you pay off your loan.

Car insurance is a big expense. It can be $75 to $100 or more a month for young people. This is in addition to your monthly car payment. The cost of insurance depends on many things. Because young people usually have more accidents than older people, they pay higher insurance rates. Men are more likely than women to have an accident, so their insurance costs more.

Expensive cars have higher insurance rates because they cost more to repair. Your driving record affects the cost of your insurance. The more accidents you have or tickets you get, the more you pay for insurance. Finally, people who live in large cities tend to have a greater chance of having an accident or having their car stolen. So, people in big cities pay more for insurance.

Reckless or Responsible

After you get a car, driving is a big responsibility. A driver should be safe and not reckless. A reckless driver takes chances, such as speeding or turning sharply in front of other cars. Reckless drivers often have accidents.

Responsible drivers realize that safe driving is a matter of life and death. They follow the traffic laws and look out for traffic signs. They know these laws and signs help cars share the road.

Did You Know ?

In some states, children under 21 can get car insurance on their parents' policies. Parents sometimes receive a discount if their child has passed a driving course or if the child has good grades in school.

Responsible drivers are also polite. They wait for their turn to pull out onto a road. They know that cutting in front of other cars causes accidents. They watch and wait until it is safe to pull out onto the road or pass another car.

Responsible drivers take care of their cars. They make sure their cars are safe to drive. They get new tires when they need them. They have their brakes checked to make sure they work well. They also make sure all their lights are working.

Saying No to Drinking and Driving

When you are driving, a mistake can cause anything from a dent in your bumper to a death. People who drink alcohol and drive greatly increase their chances of having an accident. Alcohol slows down the way people think and react. For example, if you have been drinking, you may not realize you are driving into the path of another car. You may not be able to turn your car fast enough to avoid an accident.

Remember
Never get into a car with a driver who has been drinking. A real friend stops such a person from driving.

Police watch how people are driving. If they think a driver has been drinking, they will stop the car. The police may ask a driver to take a test to see whether the driver has been drinking. It might be a breath test, which tests the alcohol level on a driver's breath. If it is over a certain amount, a driver will be considered drunk. There is also a test to see whether the driver can walk a straight line.

Drivers who refuse to take the test, or who fail it, may be arrested. Drunk drivers may lose their driver's licenses and have to pay large fines. Many are sent to jail. Never drink and drive.

Practice

On a separate sheet of paper, write at least three ways a responsible driver acts. Trade papers with a partner and compare lists.

Read the situation below. Then follow the steps to help Greg.

Think back to Greg from the beginning of the chapter. He was looking for a job. He just found a job that is a 15-minute drive from his home. Greg still does not have a car, but his city has buses. Also, one of Greg's neighbors works for the same company and has a car.

On a separate sheet of paper, follow the steps below to help Greg decide how to travel to his new job.

STEP 1   Identify the decision Greg must make.

STEP 2   List Greg's choices.

STEP 3   Cross out any choices that are harmful or might be against Greg's beliefs.

STEP 4   Think about the possible results of the remaining choices.

STEP 5   Select the best choice.

STEP 6   Explain how Greg would carry out those choices.

STEP 7   Describe the possible results of Greg's choices.

Make a Difference

What advice would you give Greg about finding a ride to work?

Summary

Many people use public transportation instead of cars to get places.
Bus schedules show the routes buses take and the times when they arrive at each stop.
To get a driver's license, you must pass a written test and a driving test.
Used cars usually cost less than new cars. However, used cars may have hidden problems and may not last as long as new cars.
When you buy a car, choose a car dealer that has a good reputation.
Many people borrow money from a bank to pay for a car. They must make monthly payments with interest to pay back the loan.
If people make loan payments late, they are charged late fees. If they stop paying, the bank may take back the car.
By law, all drivers must have car insurance.
Responsible drivers follow the traffic laws and signs.
Responsible drivers do not drink and drive.

Vocabulary Review

Write *true* or *false* after each sentence. If the sentence is false, change the underlined word or words to make it true. Use a separate sheet of paper.

1. The first payment on a large purchase is called a <u>car insurance</u>.

2. To change the oil or adjust a car's engine is to <u>route</u> it.

3. <u>Car pools</u> are groups of people who share rides in each other's cars.

4. A system of buses, trains, and subways is called <u>public transportation</u>.

5. A person who works on car engines is a <u>mechanic</u>.

Chapter Quiz

Write your answers in complete sentences.

1. What can a bus schedule tell you?

2. What should you do before you take the written test for a driver's license?

3. What do you do during the driving part of the test for a license?

4. What can you do to avoid buying a used car with problems?

5. When you buy a car with a bank loan, who owns that car? Why is that?

6. What are some things that affect the cost of car insurance?

7. **CRITICAL THINKING** How does drinking alcohol affect drivers?

Writing Activity

Why do so many teenagers want their own cars? Is having their own cars good for teenagers? Why or why not? Write your ideas on a separate sheet of paper.

Group Activity

Get a copy of the booklet that describes your state's traffic laws and signs. Using the booklet, work with a partner to make up your own written test. Write your questions on a separate sheet of paper. List ten questions on the driving laws and signs. Then trade tests with other students. See whether you can answer each other's questions correctly.

Moving into a new place to live can be challenging and exciting. What do people look for in a place to live?

Learning Objectives

- Identify housing choices.
- Describe issues to consider when renting a room or an apartment.
- Explain how to use classified ads to find an apartment.
- List what to find out before renting an apartment.
- Describe ways to furnish an apartment with little money.
- Provide tips on keeping an apartment clean.

Chapter 19 ▶ Finding Housing

Words to Know

housing	places where people live
rent	to pay an owner to live in a certain place
studio apartment	a one-room apartment
mortgage	a loan used to buy a place to live
security deposit	money that renters pay in case they damage their housing
landlord	someone who owns a house or an apartment and rents it to others
rental agreement	a written agreement between a renter and a landlord; a lease
classified ads	advertisements listed in a special section of the newspaper

One part of living on your own is finding a place to live. Someday, you might face a situation like Mei's.

Mei graduated from high school a year ago. Since then, she has been living with her family and working. Now Mei wants to get a place of her own. One of Mei's friends moved into an apartment right after high school. But now that friend has moved back with her family. She could not afford the rent. Another friend also moved out of his apartment. It was too noisy for him to study.

Mei does not want to make these mistakes. Yet she does not know how to avoid them. She needs to learn more about **housing** choices. Housing means places where people live.

19-1 ► Choosing a Place to Live

You can **rent** or buy housing. When you rent housing, you pay an owner to live in a certain place. When you buy, you own the place where you live.

Sometimes, families rent out rooms in their houses. In some houses, renters have their own bathrooms. In other houses, a renter might share a bathroom with another renter or with the family that lives there. Renters might also be allowed to use the kitchen in the home.

A **studio apartment** is usually a one-room apartment. It has a small kitchenette and a space for a bed, a couch, and some other furniture. Most studio apartments include a bathroom that is connected to the main room. A studio apartment might be in someone's house or in an apartment building. Studio apartments are also called *efficiency apartments*.

Larger apartments are named by the number of bedrooms they have. For example, a three-bedroom apartment would have three bedrooms. The number of rooms an apartment has affects the cost.

Apartments also come in different types, such as condominiums, townhouses, and family-style houses. Condominiums are apartments that people buy and own. People might rent or buy a townhouse. A townhouse usually has two floors and is connected to other townhouses on one or both sides. A single-family house is a detached house where one family lives. The family members might rent or own their house.

Eliminating Some Choices

People looking for their own place to live for the first time usually do not have much money to spend. They must think carefully about housing choices and decide what fits their budget.

Think About It

Why is a small one-room apartment sometimes called an "efficiency"?

Many people cannot afford to make a down payment of several thousand dollars on an apartment, a house, or a condominium. Buying a house or condominium means making monthly **mortgage** payments of several hundred dollars or more. A mortgage is a loan used to buy a place to live.

A mortgage is similar to a car loan. People who want to buy a house ask a bank to lend them money. If they have a good credit report and enough income, the bank may lend them the money. Then the new homeowners must pay back the money they borrowed, plus interest. They do this by making mortgage payments to the bank every month. The bank tells them what their monthly payments will be.

Renting Housing

Most people begin living on their own by renting their housing. Renters do not pay a mortgage. Instead, they pay monthly rent. Sometimes renters also have to pay their last month's rent in advance. They also pay a **security deposit** when they move in, along with the first month's rent. A security deposit is money that renters pay in case they damage the housing. If they cause damage, that money will be used to pay for repairs. If the renter does not cause any damage, the money is returned to the renter when he or she moves out. The **landlord** keeps the security deposit in case of damage. A landlord is someone who owns a house or an apartment and rents it to others. Suppose renters make a hole in a wall. The landlord would use the security deposit to pay to fix the wall.

▶ **Everyday Tip**
Take care of your apartment and keep it clean. Then you will get your whole security deposit back when you move out.

More About the Cost of Renting

The amount of rent you pay usually depends on several different things. A bigger apartment is usually more expensive than a smaller one. A new apartment in very good condition usually costs more money than an older apartment that shows some wear.

Did You Know ?

In many areas, there are flyers and newspapers that list apartments for rent.

The location of an apartment and what is included in it also affects the rent. Apartments in some areas cost more than apartments in other areas. Rents for a certain apartment may be higher because it includes parking, air conditioning, or a washer and dryer. Rent may also include the cost of heating the apartment. The more that is included, the higher the rent.

In addition to rent, you will have to pay for telephone service. You might also have to pay for electricity, gas, and water. An apartment can be very expensive.

One way to lower these costs is to share an apartment. Then each person will pay part of the rent and bills. If you do decide to share an apartment, choose someone you can trust. Find someone who will be responsible about paying bills and taking care of the apartment.

Practice

Find out the rent for three different apartments in your community. Your community might have a free booklet describing apartments in the area.

Find out the size of each apartment and what storage areas or other benefits it includes. Ask what costs are included in the rent. Share what you learn with the class.

19-2 ▶ Signing a Rental Agreement

Renters must sign a **rental agreement**, or lease. This is a written agreement between a renter and a property owner. It is signed by both. If two people share an apartment, they often both sign the rental agreement. The rental agreement usually states the amount of the rent and the security deposit you would pay, when and to whom the rent must be paid each month, who pays the electricity and water bill, and the length of the rental period. The rules that renters must follow should also be in the rental agreement.

A rental agreement is usually for a period of one year. It also states that you have to tell the landlord when you plan to move out. Sometimes a rental agreement says that renters have to pay rent for the entire period of the lease, even if they move out earlier.

Practice

Work with a partner. Role-play a landlord and a renter talking about a lease. The landlord explains the terms, and the renter asks questions about what is not covered. Write a summary of your ideas.

19-3 ▶ Finding a Place

When it is time to look for a place of your own, talk to your friends and family members for advice. Many times, the **classified ads** are the best way to help you find available apartments. These ads are in a special section of the newspaper. They list properties that are for sale or for rent.

People abbreviate words in classified ads to save space. Sometimes the same word is shortened different ways in different ads. For example, look at the ads on page 276. One ad shortens *laundry* to *laun.* Another ad shortens *laundry* to *lndry.* Here are some common abbreviations.

Abbreviations			
RM	room	apt	apartment
BR	bedroom	A/C	air conditioning
mo	month	fr	from
dep	deposit	furn.	furnished
cpt	carpeted	W/D	washer/dryer
off st. prkg	off street parking	appls.	appliances
utils.	utilities	refrig.	refrigerator
btwn	between	nr.	near

Reading classified ads is an important part of finding a place to live.

Location

Along with the rent and services, you need to think about where you want to live. You might want to live near your school or job. If you ride the bus, you might want a place near a bus stop. You also want to live in a safe neighborhood.

Most classified ads give the location of the apartment or house. For example, the ad might say *NE* for the northeast area of your city or *SW* for southwest. Some ads give the address. Booklets that list rental housing may use maps to show locations. Use this information to find places in the area where you want to live. Make a list of the ones you might consider.

If an apartment sounds good, find out where it is. Most ads include a phone number. Call and ask for the address. If the landlord will not tell you, cross that place off your list. There must be something wrong with its location.

What Else to Find Out Before You Rent

After you have several places to consider, call for information about each one. Ask whether the place is furnished. Some apartments and houses come with furniture, dishes, and even sheets and towels. However, they cost more than unfurnished places. Unfurnished places often have a stove and a refrigerator. However, you have to supply everything else you will need to live there. Think about what you will need. If there is no washing machine, find out whether there is a laundromat nearby.

Find out how much the rent and security deposit are for the apartment. The deposit might be one month's rent or more. Sometimes it is less than a month's rent. Find out what the rent includes and what costs you will have to pay yourself.

Visit the places that sound good to you. The classified ads might have left out something you really like or do not like. Many times an ad makes an apartment sound wonderful. When you go there, however, you may see that it has many problems.

See whether the outside areas are well lit. Be sure that the doors and windows have strong locks. Find out whether crime is a problem in the area. You need to feel comfortable walking around the neighborhood.

Find out what the neighbors are like. You might not make many new friends if all your neighbors are quite a bit older than you. However, if they are all young, they might be noisy.

While you are at the apartment, write down what you like and do not like about the place and the neighborhood. If you look at several places, you may soon forget which one is which. Your notes will help you remember.

Once you have gathered information, you should be ready to make a decision. Rent the place that you can afford and that you like best.

Did You Know ?

Some neighborhoods have a group called Neighborhood Watch. Volunteers walk in groups around an area at night to make sure the area stays safe.

The landlord might also have some questions for you. He or she may ask where you work and how much you earn. The landlord may ask you to prove how much you earn. He or she wants to make sure you can pay the rent. You may have to show a landlord pay stubs to prove you earn enough to cover your rent.

Practice

Choose one of the ads on page 276. Write down each abbreviation and what it means.

19-4 ▸ Furnishing Your New Home

To live in your new place, you will need something to sleep on, sit on, and eat on. There are many ways to get

Garage sales are great places to buy useful things at low prices.

what you need without spending a lot. You might ask your parents, other family members, neighbors, and friends if they have things they no longer want. Many people have furniture, dishes, and other things they no longer use. They might give them to you.

Another way to furnish a place is to buy things cheaply at garage sales, tag sales, and secondhand shops. Buying used furniture is a good way to get started. You could also save money by thinking of new ways to use the furniture you have. Use a card table for a kitchen table. Use your bed as a couch during the day. The less you spend on furniture, the more you can save for the future.

Practice

Write a list of things someone would need for a small apartment. Make sure to remember pots and pans, towels, lighting, and cleaning supplies. Combine your list with others to make one class list.

19-5 ▸ Taking Care of Your Home

If you take care of your place, you will feel more comfortable there. Cleaning is easy if you have the right tools. Be sure to get sponges, a toilet brush, a broom and dustpan, a mop, and a bucket. If you have a carpet, get a vacuum cleaner. Also, buy cleaning products such as soap for the dishes, detergent for clothes, and cleaners for the bathroom.

Cleaning is also easier if you set up a schedule. Then you are less likely to forget to clean. Some things should be done every day. Wash the dishes and wipe off the table and kitchen counters. Sweep or vacuum the kitchen floor so crumbs do not attract bugs. When you put away clothes and shoes and make your bed every day, your apartment will look neater.

You will need to do some things at least once a week. Change the towels in the bathroom. Sweep or vacuum all the floors. Remember to take out the garbage. Change the bed sheets and clean the bathroom, including the toilet. Dust the furniture and wash the kitchen floor.

Practice

On a separate sheet of paper, list the pros and cons of having your own place to live. Look at your list and decide whether living on your own sounds exciting or difficult.

Washing dishes is part of keeping your home clean.

YOU DECIDE
How to Find the Right Place to Live

Read the situation below. Then help Mei decide on the right place to live.

Think back to Mei from the beginning of the chapter. She was thinking of getting a place of her own. Her friend Elise has an apartment and wants Mei to live with her. However, the apartment is not near a bus stop. Mei does not have a car. She would have a long walk to catch a bus.

On a separate sheet of paper, follow the steps below to help Mei decide what to do.

STEP 1 Identify the decision Mei must make.

STEP 2 List Mei's choices.

STEP 3 Cross out any choices that are harmful or might be against Mei's beliefs.

STEP 4 Think about the remaining choices.

STEP 5 Select the best choice.

STEP 6 Explain how Mei would carry that choice out.

STEP 7 Describe the possible results.

Make a Difference
What advice would you give Mei about sharing an apartment with Elise?

19 ╱ Review

Summary

Housing includes room rentals of different sizes, townhouses, condominiums, and houses.
Buying housing requires a down payment and a monthly mortgage payment.
Young people usually start out by renting a room or an apartment. They pay a security deposit and monthly rent. They also sign a rental agreement.
The opinions of friends and classified ads can help you find a place to live.
Consider the rent, size, and location of each place. Ask what is included. Consider safety in the neighborhood and in laundry and parking areas.
You can furnish your place by asking friends and family for things they no longer use. You can also shop at garage sales and secondhand shops.
To care for an apartment, buy cleaning supplies, set up a cleaning schedule, and clean the apartment regularly.

Vocabulary Review

rent

mortgage

housing

classified ads

security deposit

landlord

studio apartment

rental agreement

Write the term from the list that matches each definition below. Use a separate sheet of paper.

1. one-room apartment

2. owner of a house or an apartment who rents it to others

3. advertisements listed in a special section of the newspaper

4. lease

5. places in which people live

6. loan used to buy a place to live

7. money that renters pay in case they damage their housing

8. pay an owner to live in a certain place

Chapter Quiz

Write your answers in complete sentences.

1. What kinds of payments may be required to buy a house or condominium?

2. What kinds of payments should renters expect to make?

3. What things affect the rent for an apartment or house?

4. What information is included in a rental agreement?

5. How can you get furniture for your new place?

6. Why is it helpful to have a cleaning schedule?

7. **CRITICAL THINKING** Why is the location of a place to live important?

Writing Activity

Suppose you have a cousin who is graduating from high school next year. This cousin is thinking about getting an apartment. Make up details about your cousin's life and needs. On a separate sheet of paper, write your cousin a letter. Explain whether you think he or she should get an apartment. Explain why.

Group Activity

With a group, list at least five skills you are learning in school that will help you live on your own. One example is math skills, which you can use to figure out whether you can afford an apartment. Then list things you have not learned that you need to know. Share both lists with the class. Talk about how you could find the information or learn the skills you still need.

Unit 6 **Review**

Read each sentence below. Then choose the letter that best completes each one.

1. People use public transportation to
   A. go to school.
   B. go to work.
   C. visit friends.
   D. all of the above

2. Housing choices include all of the following, except
   A. apartments.
   B. resorts.
   C. rooms.
   D. condominiums.

3. Used cars usually
   A. cost more than new cars.
   B. have fewer miles than new cars.
   C. cost less than new cars.
   D. last longer than new cars.

4. You should consider all of the following when looking for a place to live, except
   A. the wall colors.
   B. the location.
   C. the size.
   D. the rent.

5. When most people buy a car, they can
   A. make a down payment.
   B. decide the cost of monthly payments.
   C. not pay for several months.
   D. all of the above

6. One way to care for an apartment is to
   A. leave dirty dishes in a sink.
   B. clean regularly.
   C. leave clothes all over the apartment.
   D. avoid vacuuming or dusting.

Critical Thinking
Stella is taking the bus to work and saving her money for a car. Kim already bought a very old car with a little money she had saved. Which girl do you think made the better decision? Why?
WRITING Suppose you read a classified ad about an apartment that sounded great. Write a list of steps you would take next to decide if this place was right for you.

Unit **7** **You and Your Community**

Serving on a jury is an important part of being a good citizen. Why do you think that is so?

Learning Objectives

- Explain the purpose of a Social Security card.
- Explain how to register to vote.
- Describe how to learn more about candidates.
- Identify what taxes are.
- Explain what to do if you receive a jury summons.
- Describe volunteer opportunities in the community.

Chapter 20 › Being a Good Citizen

Words to Know

citizen	someone who lives in a certain city or nation
maiden name	a woman's last name before she is married
register	to sign up to vote
issue	a question people make a decision on
candidate	a person running for an office in an election
income tax	money that everyone who works pays to the government
federal	national
tax deduction	a cost that can be subtracted from your income when you figure out your taxes
standard deduction	an amount of money set by the government for each income level; it can be subtracted from your income
exemption	a tax deduction for each person in a family
withheld	held back; taken out
jury	a group of people chosen to decide whether someone on trial is innocent or guilty
summons	a legal request

Read Kim's conversation with Henry about voting.

"Who do you want for president?" Henry asked.

"Vote?" Kim said. "I'm not going to vote. It's too hard to sign up to vote. I hate filling out forms. I don't even know what the election is about."

Kim is not being a good **citizen.** A citizen is someone who lives in a certain city or nation. Being a good citizen means doing your part and taking an active role. Good citizens vote. They pay their taxes, serve on juries, and volunteer their time to the community. In addition, they obey the laws. This chapter and the next one explain how to be a good citizen.

20-1 ▸ Getting a Social Security Card

▶ **Everyday Tip**
Always keep your Social
Security card in a safe place.

Part of being a citizen is getting a Social Security card. Your parents might have gotten one for you when you were born. Children born in the United States must have a Social Security card before they are one year old.

What is really important about a Social Security card is the number on your card. You are the only person who will have that number. You will probably have the same number for your entire life. You will need this number when you apply for many things, such as credit cards and loans. Many forms ask for this number.

When you start working, you will need your Social Security number. Employers use the numbers to report each person's income to the government.

If you are under 18 and do not have a Social Security number, your parents should get one for you. If you are over 18, you must apply at a Social Security office for a number. These offices are listed in the government pages of the telephone book. Look under U.S. Government, Social Security Administration. There is no cost for getting a Social Security number.

When you apply for your Social Security number, you need to prove who you are. Take your original birth certificate and one other form of identification. This could be your driver's license or a school ID. If you were not born in the United States, you will need your foreign birth certificate or passport and the papers you received from the Immigration and Naturalization Service.

SOCIAL SECURITY ADMINISTRATION
Application for a Social Security Card

Form approved
OMB No.0960-0066

Instructions

- Please read "How To Complete This Form" on page 2.
- Print or type using black or blue ink. DO NOT USE PENCIL.
- After you complete this form, take or mail it along with the required documents to your nearest Social Security office.
- If you are completing this form for someone else, answer the questions as they apply to that person. Then, sign your name in question 16.

1 NAME
To Be Shown On Card

▶ FIRST   FULL MIDDLE NAME   LAST

FULL NAME AT BIRTH
IF OTHER THAN ABOVE

FIRST   FULL MIDDLE NAME   LAST

2 MAILING ADDRESS
Do Not Abbreviate

▶ STREET ADDRESS, APT. NO., PO BOX, RURAL ROUTE NO.

CITY   STATE   ZIP CODE

3 CITIZENSHIP
(check one)

☐ U.S. Citizen   ☐ Legal Alien Allowed To Work   ☐ Legal Alien Not Allowed To Work   ☐ Foreign Student Allowed Restricted Employment   ☐ Conditionally Legalized Alien Allowed To Work   ☐ Other (See Instructions On Page 2)

4 SEX   ☐ Male   ☐ Female

5 RACE/ETHNIC DESCRIPTION

☐ Asian, Asian American Or Pacific Islander   ☐ Hispanic   ☐ Black (Not Hispanic)   ☐ North American Indian Or Alaskan Native   ☐ White (Not Hispanic)

6 DATE OF BIRTH ____ MONTH DAY YEAR

7 PLACE OF BIRTH
Do Not Abbreviate   CITY   STATE OR FOREIGN COUNTRY

Office Use Only   FCI

8 MOTHER'S MAIDEN NAME

FIRST   FULL MIDDLE NAME   LAST NAME AT HER BIRTH

9 FATHER'S NAME

FIRST   FULL MIDDLE NAME   LAST

10 Has the person in item 1 ever received a Social Security number before?

☐ Yes (If "yes", answer questions 11–13.)   ☐ No (If "no", go on to question 14.)   ☐ Don't Know (If "don't know", go on to question 14.)

11 Enter the Social Security number previously assigned to the person listed in item 1.

☐☐☐–☐☐–☐☐☐☐

12 Enter the name shown on the most recent Social Security card issued for the person in item 1.

FIRST   MIDDLE   LAST

13 Enter any different date of birth if used on an earlier application for a card.

MONTH DAY YEAR

14 TODAY'S DATE ▶ MONTH DAY YEAR

15 DAYTIME PHONE NUMBER ▶ ( ) AREA CODE

DELIBERATELY FURNISHING (OR CAUSING TO BE FURNISHED) FALSE INFORMATION ON THIS APPLICATION IS A CRIME PUNISHABLE BY FINE OR IMPRISONMENT, OR BOTH

16 YOUR SIGNATURE

▶

17 YOUR RELATIONSHIP TO THE PERSON IN ITEM 1 IS: ☐ Self   ☐ Natural Or Adoptive Parent   ☐ Legal Guardian   ☐ Other (Specify)

DO NOT WRITE BELOW THIS LINE (FOR SSA USE ONLY)

NPN			DOC	NTI	CAN		ITV
PBC	EVI	EVA	EVC	PRA	NWR	DNR	UNIT
EVIDENCE SUBMITTED				SIGNATURE AND TITLE OF EMPLOYEE(S) REVIEWING EVIDENCE AND/OR CONDUCTING INTERVIEW			
							DATE
				DCL			DATE

Form SS-5 (9/89) 5/88 edition may be used until supply is exhausted

This is the form to fill out to get your Social Security number.

To get a Social Security card, you will have to fill out a form like the one on page 289. The form asks for basic information about you. It asks for your name, address, citizenship, and sex, and the date and place of your birth. It also asks for your father's name and your mother's **maiden name.** A maiden name is a woman's last name before she is married. If you lose your card, you will have to fill out the form again. You must also prove who you are again. To replace a lost card, you can use a driver's license, school record, passport, or health insurance card for identification.

Practice

Look over the Social Security card application form shown on page 289. On a separate sheet of paper, fill in all the information you would put on the form.

20-2 ▶ Registering to Vote

Another part of being a good citizen is voting. In every state except North Dakota you must **register** before you can vote. To register means to sign up to vote. When you register to vote, you fill out a voter registration form. To register, you must be a citizen of the United States and at least 18 years old.

It is easy to register to vote. You can register to vote at any Bureau of Motor Vehicles office. You can also register to vote by mail. You can get a registration form at most post offices and libraries, and at the Board of Elections office. You must mail the form to the address printed on the form.

Each time you move, you should register to vote. Every state has its own rules about how and when to register. Find out the rules in your state. You can call the Board of Elections for registration information.

After you register, the Board of Elections will mail you a Voter Registration Card. You will be assigned a place to vote near your home. It might be a school or a library. On election day, go to that place, show your Voter Registration Card, and sign your name. Then you can vote.

In the United States, your vote is secret. No one will know who you vote for. You have the right to vote for any person you choose. Remember, you do not have to tell anyone how you voted.

Voting Choices

When you vote, you help shape the government. You help choose your own leaders, such as mayor, governor, senator, and president. To be a good citizen, you need to know who the candidates in each election are and what they stand for.

You might also vote on **issues.** An issue is a question that people make a decision on. For example, you might be asked to vote on whether there should be a new tax to pay for a new school.

Preparing to Vote

Just before an election, you will see many advertisements on television, hear them on the radio, and read them in newspapers. These ads will try to get you to vote in a certain way.

Remember
Look closely at ads. Ads use many ways to influence your thinking.

Ads only give you one side of an issue. They try to make one **candidate** look good and the others look bad. A candidate is someone who is running for an office, such as mayor or president, in an election.

Before you vote, gather information. Be sure to read materials that give the facts but do not tell you how to vote. Consider your choices carefully. Then you can make your own wise decision. Avoid letting anyone decide who you should vote for. Your vote is your decision.

Practice

Read the ad below for a new school tax called Issue 37. Then, answer the questions on a separate sheet of paper.

★ ★

VOTE for ISSUE 37

The future is in your hands. Without your help, our children will spend their days in school buildings that are falling apart. **A vote for Issue 37 is a vote for our community's future!**

1. What facts does this ad give?

2. What else would you want to know before you voted for or against Issue 37?

20-3 ▸ Paying Taxes

All citizens benefit from the services that tax money buys for our communities. Money from taxes pays for police officers, firefighters, roads, parks, and schools. Taxes also pay part of the costs of community and state colleges.

Income tax is money that everyone who works pays to the government. The amount of tax people pay is based on their income. Income is the amount of money a person earns. People pay income taxes to the city, state, and **federal** government. Federal is another word for national. The federal government is the United States government.

It is against the law to refuse to pay income taxes. People who do not pay their income taxes can go to jail.

Tax Deductions

You do not have to pay taxes on all the money you earn. Everyone gets a **tax deduction.** Tax deductions are costs that you have paid during the year. You can subtract these costs from your income when you figure out your taxes. Then you owe taxes on the amount of income that is left. Some common tax deductions include city and state income tax, property taxes, and donations to religious groups and charities.

You can list each deduction on your tax return. However, many people do not. Instead, they take a **standard deduction.** The standard deduction is a certain amount of money determined by the government each year for each income level.

In 2000, the standard deduction was $4,400 for a single person. It was $7,350 for a married couple filing jointly.

Exemptions

Workers can also subtract money from their incomes for **exemptions.** An exemption is a tax deduction for members of your family. You get one exemption for each person in your family whom you support. In 2000, the amount for each exemption was $2,800.

You get one exemption for yourself. Married couples get two exemptions—one for each person. A single parent or a married couple get one exemption for each child. Here is how a single person could use the standard deduction and one exemption.

Income	$20,000
Standard deduction	−4,400
One exemption	−2,800
	$12,800

This person would owe taxes on $12,800. Based on a tax ratio of 15 percent, that is about $1,920.

Think About It

How do you think deductions and exemptions help a taxpayer?

Withholding

During the year, your employer subtracts income tax from each of your paychecks. Then in January, your employer sends you a W-2 form. This form shows the amount of money you earned during the past year. It also shows the amount of income tax that has already been **withheld** from your paychecks. Withheld means held back or taken out.

Because of the system of withholding, most of your income taxes have already been paid. All you need to pay is the amount you still owe. Some people have more income tax withheld than they owe. After filling out their tax forms, they will receive tax refunds that give them back the extra money they paid.

a Control number		Void ☐	For Official Use Only OMB No. 1545-0008	
b Employer identification number			**1** Wages, tips, other compensation	**2** Federal income tax withheld
c Employer's name, address, and ZIP code			**3** Social security wages	**4** Social security tax withheld
			5 Medicare wages and tips	**6** Medicare tax withheld
			7 Social security tips	**8** Allocated tips
d Employee's social security number			**9** Advance EIC payment	**10** Dependent care benefits
e Employee's name, address, and ZIP code			**11** Nonqualified plans	**12** Benefits included in box 1
			13 See instr. for box 13	**14** Other
			15 Statutory employee ☐ Deceased ☐ Pension plan ☐ Legal rep. ☐ Deferred compensation ☐	
16 State Employer's state I.D. no.	**17** State wages, tips, etc.	**18** State income tax	**19** Locality name **20** Local wages, tips, etc.	**21** Local income tax

Form **W-2 Wage and Tax Statement 2000**   Copy **B** To Be Filed With Employee's Federal Tax Form   Dept. of Treasury—IRS

The W-2 form shows you the amount of money you earned during the year. Here is a blank copy of a W-2 form.

Practice

On a separate sheet of paper, figure out the amount of taxes James and his wife June owed in 2000. James earned $17,000 that year. They took the standard deduction for a married couple. Their tax rate was 15 percent.

Filing a Tax Form

Once you have filed a tax form, the Internal Revenue Service (IRS) sends you a tax form each year. You can also get forms at the library or at the post office or another government office. The tax form is really a worksheet.

Each tax form has a place to list your income. It tells you to subtract your deductions and exemptions. Tables in the instruction booklet help you figure out what you owe. Reading the instruction booklet carefully will help you fill out your tax return.

You must complete your tax form each year and send it to the IRS by April 15. If you have trouble filling out the forms, get help. Libraries have instruction booklets and tapes. You can also call the IRS using the toll-free phone number on your tax booklet. Some businesses will also fill out the forms for you. However, they charge a fee. Look under *Tax Preparation* in the Yellow Pages.

Using Technology

You can get income tax forms online at www.irs.gov. This is very helpful if you need extra copies of a form.

Practice

On a separate sheet of paper, list three ways you can get help in preparing your income tax form.

				Dollars	Cents
Income **Attach Form(s) W-2 here.** Enclose, but do not staple, any payment.	**1**	Total wages, salaries, and tips. This should be shown in box 1 of your W-2 form(s). Attach your W-2 form(s).	1		
	2	Taxable interest. If the total is over $400, you cannot use Form 1040EZ.	2		
	3	Unemployment compensation, qualified state tuition program earnings, and Alaska Permanent Fund dividends (see page 14).	3		
	4	Add lines 1, 2, and 3. This is your **adjusted gross income.**	4		
Note. You **must** check } Yes or No.	**5**	Can your parents (or someone else) claim you on their return? **Yes.** Enter amount from ☐ worksheet on back. **No.** If **single**, enter 7,200.00. ☐ If **married**, enter 12,950.00. See back for explanation.	5		
	6	Subtract line 5 from line 4. If line 5 is larger than line 4, enter 0. This is your **taxable income.** ▶	6		

This is part of the 1040EZ form for 2000.

Serving on a Jury and Volunteering

In the United States, each person who is accused of a crime has the right to a trial. During the trial, a **jury**, or a group of people chosen to determine a person's innocence or guilt, listens to both sides of the case. Then the jury decides whether the person is innocent or guilty. Serving on a jury is a duty of a good citizen.

Some day you may get a **summons** for jury duty. A summons is a legal request. It will tell you when and where you must appear for jury duty. If you cannot be there, call the phone number on the summons. If you ignore a summons, you may get into serious trouble.

People are excused from jury duty only for serious reasons. If you are called for jury duty, your employer must give you time off from work. Jurors receive a small amount of money for each day they serve.

If you have been called for jury duty, be sure to arrive on time. The judge or lawyers who are part of a trial might ask you questions. They might decide to excuse you, or let you go, from jury duty for any number of reasons. If you are chosen for a jury, listen closely during the trial. Then when you are asked to make a decision, think carefully about what you heard.

Volunteering is another way to be a good citizen. There are many ways to do this, such as cutting a neighbor's grass or helping deliver meals to elderly people.

You have many opportunities to be a good citizen. Some are required, like paying taxes or serving on a jury. Others you can choose, like voting and volunteering.

Did You Know

Many people are called to jury duty only once or twice in their lifetimes. Sometimes they do not even make it onto a jury.

Practice

Talk with a small group of your classmates. Think of ways to volunteer in your community. Then share your group's ideas with the class. Try out one of your ideas.

YOU DECIDE
How to Choose a Candidate

Read the story below. Then follow the steps to help Sam make a wise decision.

Sam's neighbor, Milo Stanfield, is running for the school board. He has asked Sam and his family to vote for him. Sam thinks Milo Stanfield is a nice person. However, Milo wants to increase local property taxes to build another high school. He thinks the school has too many students. Sam does not know the other candidate. However, he does know she is against raising taxes.

On a separate sheet of paper, follow the steps below to help Sam decide which person to vote for.

STEP 1   Identify the decision Sam must make.

STEP 2   List Sam's choices.

STEP 3   Cross out any choices that are harmful or might be against Sam's beliefs.

STEP 4   Think about the possible results of the remaining choices.

STEP 5   Select the best choice.

STEP 6   Explain how Sam would carry out that choice.

STEP 7   Describe the possible results of Sam's choice.

Make a Difference

What advice would you give Sam about which candidate to vote for?

Chapter

20 Review

Summary

Everyone has to have a Social Security number. It is used as a form of identification for your whole life. You need it for many things, including loans and credit cards.

To apply for a Social Security card, you must go to a Social Security office. Take two forms of identification.

Voting is part of being a good citizen. You can register to vote at any Bureau of Motor Vehicles office. You can also register by mail.

Before you vote, learn about the candidates and the issues.

Money from income taxes pays for many community services. These include schools, highways, and fire protection services.

Income tax forms help you figure out what you owe. Use a tax instruction booklet to fill out the form.

If you receive a jury summons, follow the directions on it. Serving on a jury is a serious matter and part of being a good citizen.

Volunteering is another way to be a good citizen.

Vocabulary Review

citizen

exemption

maiden name

register

summons

federal

Complete each sentence with a term from the list. Use a separate sheet of paper.

1. To sign up to vote is to ____.
2. A tax deduction for each person in a family is an ____.
3. The word ____ means national.
4. Someone who lives in a certain city or nation is a ____.
5. A legal request is a ____.
6. A woman's last name before she is married is her ____.

Chapter Quiz

Write your answers in complete sentences.

1. Where can you apply for a Social Security number?

2. How do you register to vote?

3. What is a tax deduction? What is an exemption?

4. Where could you find help in filling out your income tax form?

5. If you receive a jury summons, will you be part of a jury? Why or why not?

6. What are three ways that young people in your community can volunteer their time?

7. **CRITICAL THINKING** Julio did not know anything about the candidates or the issues. But he wants to vote anyway. What should he do? Why?

Writing Activity

Sometimes people do not like the way the government spends their tax money. What are some ways ordinary people can influence how the government spends money? On a separate sheet of paper, write your ideas in a letter to your representative in Congress.

Group Activity

Get a copy of the current 1040EZ tax form. Work with a small group to create a taxpayer who has no children. A taxpayer with children cannot use this form. Decide on the taxpayer's income and whether he or she is married. Then fill out the form by following the instructions on the back.

Part of being a good citizen is doing things that benefit the community. What are some things that you can do to benefit your community?

Learning Objectives

- Identify traffic laws.
- Describe steps to take if you have a car accident.
- Explain safety rules for riding a bicycle.
- Explain laws about curfews, littering, and calling in a false alarm.

Words to Know

traffic	the movement of people and vehicles through an area
fine	a fee a person must pay for breaking a law
defensive driving	driving carefully to avoid accidents
pedestrian	someone who is walking, running, or jogging
curfew	a time by which people must be home or off public property
public property	streets, highways, parks, playgrounds, and buildings that are open to all people
littering	leaving garbage on public property or on someone else's property
false alarm	a warning about a danger that is not real

Read the story below to see what happened to Jake.

Manuel drove to Jake's apartment. Jake was waiting for him, holding a bag full of garbage. "What are you going to do with that?" Manuel asked.

"Let's stop at the park," Jake said. "I'm going to put it in the park's trash can. The trash cans at my apartment building are full. Parks are for everyone, so I can use them any way I want."

A few days later, a police officer gave Jake a ticket for littering. Park employees had found Jake's name on some mail in the bag and called the police. "It's against the law to leave garbage from your home on public property," the officer explained.

You know that it is against the law to steal or to hurt other people. However, there are other laws you might not know about. This chapter will explore some of those laws. You are responsible for knowing the laws. When you know the laws, you can work to avoid getting into trouble.

21-1 ▶ Knowing the Traffic Laws

Remember
Your driver's license is a form of identification.

If you have your driver's license, you should know most of the **traffic** laws. Traffic means the movement of people and vehicles through an area. Some things that are covered by traffic laws include how fast you can drive a car on certain streets and highways, when you can pass another car, and when you must stop. Traffic laws also tell whether you can make a right turn when a traffic light is red and what to do at an intersection that has four stop signs.

Most states have a booklet that explains the traffic laws. This is the same booklet that you study to get your driver's license. You can get a copy of this booklet at any Bureau of Motor Vehicles.

Practice

Answer the questions below on a separate sheet of paper. You might get help from someone who knows the traffic laws. You could check the booklet about traffic laws from the Bureau of Motor Vehicles. Share what you learn with the class.

1. What should drivers do at railroad crossings?

2. What should drivers do when an ambulance is coming?

3. What should drivers do if a school bus stops in front of them with lights flashing?

21-2 Avoiding Traffic Tickets and Accidents

You can avoid getting a traffic ticket by obeying the law. For example, many tickets are given for speeding. No one is forced to speed. People do it because they want to go faster. Some people receive tickets for not stopping at stop signs. Others get tickets for parking in the wrong place.

The front of a traffic ticket explains which law was broken. It will also show your **fine.** A fine is a fee a person must pay for breaking a law. The back of the ticket describes how to pay the fine. Drivers under the age of 18 might have to go to traffic court with a parent to pay the fine. Older drivers might be able to pay their fines through the mail.

Using Technology

The police use new technology to help enforce the law. For example, radar guns tell police how fast a car is going.

If you get a ticket, follow the directions on the back of it. Do not ignore the ticket. Do not throw it away. If you do, you will be in more trouble. You could lose your license and have to pay a bigger fine.

Many states give drivers points as penalties for breaking the law. For example, drivers might get two points for their first speeding ticket. They might get two to six points for their second speeding ticket in the same year. The faster the drivers are going, the more points they will receive on their driving record. Drivers might receive up to 12 points for their third speeding ticket in the same year. Drivers who receive 12 points within two years often have their licenses taken away for six months or more.

Drivers also receive points for breaking the law in other ways. These include drinking and driving, and leaving the scene of an accident without calling the police.

Accidents

Unfortunately, you cannot avoid all accidents by driving carefully. Sometimes other drivers run into you, no matter what you do. However, there are many things you can do to avoid accidents. You can watch what other drivers are doing. Then you will be ready if another driver does something unexpected, such as suddenly cutting in front of you. You can also take a course in **defensive driving.** Defensive driving means driving carefully to avoid accidents.

If you have an accident, stop and see whether anyone is hurt. If so, get help. Have someone call an ambulance. Try to warn other drivers away from the accident so they will not run into your cars.

Call the police or highway patrol to report the accident. While you are waiting for the police, exchange information with the other driver. Ask for the driver's name, address, and phone number. Write down the car's license plate number, the person's driver's license number, the name of his or her insurance company, and the name of the car owner. When the police arrive, answer the police officer's questions about the accident. Do not blame the other driver for the accident, but try not to blame yourself either. The police will usually decide who is to blame.

If you are in an accident, stay calm and call the police.

You may have to fill out an accident report. Ask the police officer whether you need to do this. If a report is required, the police officer can tell you where you need to go to get the form. If you do not report an accident, you may lose your license.

If you hit a parked car, call the police and report the accident. You will have to fill out an accident report. If you do not report the accident, you could be charged with hit-and-run. Then you would be in more trouble. Finally, report the accident to your car insurance company as soon as you can.

Practice

On a separate sheet of paper, list at least five things you should do if you have an accident.

21-3 Knowing Laws for Bikers and Pedestrians

Many young people ride their bikes to get places and just for fun. Below are some basic laws for bike riders. Your state may have other laws. Most states require bike riders to wear helmets.

- Ride on the right, in the same direction cars travel. Stay on the edge of the road.
- Obey all traffic signals.
- Use hand signals when you stop or turn.
- Never ride your bike on major highways.
- Do not let anyone ride on your handlebars.
- If you ride after dark, make sure your bike has a headlight, a taillight, and red reflectors.
- Fasten a loud bell or horn to your bike.
- Make sure your brakes work.

Wearing a helmet when you ride can save your life.

A **pedestrian** is someone who is walking, running, or jogging. All people are pedestrians at one time or another. We all need to know the laws. Walking is good for you. However, it should also be safe.

Car drivers and bike riders can get tickets for not obeying the laws, and so can pedestrians. Most communities have a law that you can cross a street only at a corner or crosswalk. If you cross in the wrong place, you are jaywalking. It is against the law.

On the corners of some busy streets you may see a button you can push to change the traffic light. If you want to cross the street, you can push this button to stop traffic. Watch the sign on the other corner. Wait until the sign says "Walk." It may take a moment for the sign to change. Then you can cross the street.

You should walk, run, or jog on the sidewalk. If there is no sidewalk, walk, run, or jog on the side of the road. Stay off major highways except in an emergency. You should never hitchhike.

Practice

Draw a road on each of two separate sheets of paper. On each road, draw cars driving in both directions. On one of your drawings, add a bike rider. On the other drawing, add a pedestrian. Show both the bike rider and the pedestrian following safety laws. Compare your drawings with others in the class. Do you all agree on where the rider and pedestrian should be on the road?

21-4 ▶ Knowing Other Laws

Your community has other laws that may affect you. Some communities have a **curfew** law. A curfew is the time by which people must be home or off **public property**. Public property includes streets and highways, parks, playgrounds, and buildings that are open to all people. Some curfew laws may also include public places such as theaters and shopping malls.

For example, those under the age of 18 might have an 11:00 P.M. curfew. They would have to be off public property after 11:00 P.M. Those under the age of 14 might have a 9:00 P.M. curfew. They would have to be off public property after 9:00 P.M. Young people who are with a responsible adult are not affected by these curfews.

Most communities have **littering** laws. Littering means leaving trash on public property or on someone else's property. People can get a ticket for throwing trash on the ground.

Remember Jake from the beginning of the chapter? He found out the hard way that his community had a law against littering. Jake had put his garbage in a plastic bag. Yet he still was not allowed to put it in the park's

Think About It

Why might a curfew law be a good idea?

Cleaning up litter in a local park is one way to keep your community a pleasant place in which to live.

trash cans. You can use the park's trash cans after you have a picnic in the park. However, you cannot bring trash from home and throw it in the park's trash cans.

It is also against the law to make a **false alarm**. A false alarm is a warning about a danger that is not real. One example is yelling "Fire!" in a mall or theater when you know there is no fire. People can panic and get hurt in these situations. That is why it is against the law.

Staying Out of Trouble

Laws were made to help people get along with one another. Laws help thousands of cars use the same highways. Laws help drivers, bike riders, and pedestrians share the streets. Laws also help people live close together peacefully.

Practice

On a separate sheet of paper, discuss two laws that are important for the safety of your community. How do these laws help?

How to Report an Accident

Read the paragraphs below. Then follow the steps to help Tamika make a decision.

On her way home from work, Tamika tried to stop at a red light. The roads were icy, and she slid into the car in front of her. She and the other driver got out. Neither one was hurt, but Tamika had made a large dent in the other car. However, the other driver knew the roads were slippery. He did not seem angry. They exchanged names and other information.

After he drove away, Tamika remembered that accidents should be reported to the police. However, no one was hurt, and now the other driver was gone. Tamika could not decide whether she should call the police and report the accident.

On a separate sheet of paper, follow the steps below. Help Tamika make this decision.

STEP 1   Identify the decision Tamika must make.

STEP 2   List Tamika's choices.

STEP 3   Cross out any choices that are harmful or might be against Tamika's beliefs.

STEP 4   Think about the possible results of the remaining choices.

STEP 5   Select the best choice.

STEP 6   Explain how Tamika would carry out that choice.

STEP 7   Describe the possible results of Tamika's choices.

Make a Difference

What advice would you give Tamika about calling the police and reporting the accident?

Summary

It is important to know the traffic laws. The Bureau of Motor Vehicles can give you a booklet that explains the laws.
Careful, responsible drivers can avoid getting traffic tickets.
If you have a car accident, stop and get help if anyone is injured. Call the police to report the accident. Exchange information with the other driver. Report the accident to your insurance company.
Bike riders should ride on the right edge of the road and obey traffic signs. They should also use hand signals, stay off major highways, and not let anyone ride on their handlebars. Bikes should have lights for riding after dark, a bell or horn, and good brakes.
Pedestrians should cross streets only at corners and crosswalks. They should follow the traffic signals. Pedestrians should never hitchhike.
Many communities have laws about curfews, littering, making false alarms, and other actions.

Vocabulary Review

Write *true* or *false* after each sentence. If the statement is false, change the underlined word or words to make it true. Use a separate sheet of paper.

1. The movement of people and vehicles through an area is called <u>littering</u>.

2. Driving carefully to avoid accidents is <u>defensive driving</u>.

3. A warning about a danger that is not real is a <u>curfew</u>.

4. Someone who is walking, running, or jogging is a <u>pedestrian</u>.

5. A fee a person must pay for breaking a law is a <u>fine</u>.

6. Streets, parks, playgrounds, and buildings that are open to all people are called <u>public property</u>.

Chapter Quiz

Write your answers in complete sentences.

1. If you are not sure about a traffic law, how could you find out about it?

2. Colleen got a ticket for parking in front of a fire hydrant. She threw the ticket away. What problems could this cause for Colleen?

3. When do you have to fill out an accident report?

4. If you have an accident, what kinds of information should you exchange with the other driver?

5. What are three rules of safe bike riding?

6. You want to cross an intersection that has a traffic light. The light for the cars in the cross street is green. Should you cross the street? Why or why not?

7. **CRITICAL THINKING** Why are laws important? Think about what you learned in this chapter.

Writing Activity

Sylvia was angry about her speeding ticket. "I had to hurry to get to my doctor's appointment. I had to drive fast," she told her friends. Do you think it was fair for Sylvia to get a speeding ticket? Why or why not? Write your ideas in a paragraph on a separate sheet of paper.

Group Activity

Work with a small group to make a plan for teaching safety rules. First, decide whether to teach rules for walking or for riding bikes. Then think of a way to teach these rules. For example, your group might create posters or skits. Share your work with your class.

Community help is there if you know how to find it. What kinds of services are offered in your community?

Learning Objectives

- Locate sources of help in the telephone book.
- Explain how to find out which government agency deals with a certain problem.
- Describe a TTY (text telephone yoke).
- Explain bus services.
- Give examples of activities and services offered in the community.

Chapter 22 ▷ Finding Help in the Community

Words to Know

food stamps	coupons issued by the government that can be used to buy food
agency	a department or office that works on certain issues
TTY	text telephone yoke; equipment that helps people with speech or hearing problems use the telephone
recreation	activities to do for fun
CD-ROM database	a computer laser disk filled with an enormous amount of information

Read the paragraphs below about Carly's family to see what kinds of help Carly's family needs.

Carly, her brother Mike, and their mother just moved into a small house in a new town. Carly's mother has to find out how to get the food stamps her family needs. She also needs to arrange for phone service, because her daughter has a special need. Carly has a hearing loss, which makes talking over the phone difficult. Carly's mother wants to make sure that Carly can use the phone when she needs to.

Carly's mother also needs to find out which bus to take to look for a new job, and Mike wants to know what there is to do in the area.

Maybe you need help, like Carly's family, or maybe you just need something to do, like Mike. This chapter can help in both cases. You will learn about the services that are available in many communities.

22-1 ▸ Finding Community Services

You probably already have a list of the services in your community. It is in your telephone book. Look in the front of the white pages. You should find a section with a title such as Easy Reference List, or Community Services, or Frequently Called Numbers.

In this section, you should find phone numbers to help with a variety of problems. For example, you can find out where to report child abuse. You can also find out how to get help with other kinds of problems in the home.

▶ **Everyday Tip**
When you find a number you need to call often, keep it written near your phone. Then you will not have to look it up again.

You can use this section of the phone book to find out how to get help with a drug problem or legal problems. The listings have numbers for places to help you get free or low-cost help if you are sick or are having mental health problems.

If you need to know how to get gas, water, electric, or phone service like Carly's mother, you can find it in this section. You can also find information about services for senior citizens, voting, and elections.

Practice

Look in your phone book for a list of community services. On a separate sheet of paper, write down at least four sources of help in your community. Include the phone numbers to call.

22-2 ▸ Finding Help from the Government

Carly's family moved because her mother had lost her job. While Carly's mother looked for a new job, the family was getting **food stamps.** Food stamps are coupons issued by the government to people below a certain income level. They can be used to buy food.

If you want to know whether you can get food stamps, you need to call the right government **agency.** An agency is a department or office that works on certain issues. However, you probably do not know which agency to call. It might be part of the city, county, state, or federal government.

Your phone book can help. Some phone books have a section called "Frequently Requested Government Offices." This is a chart that shows which agency to call for certain information. For example, the chart shows that food stamps are handled by county governments.

Maybe your phone book does not have this chart. It probably does have a section for government phone numbers. The pages in this section might be blue or have blue edges. The government offices in this section are usually listed in the order shown below.

- City and town offices

- County or parish offices

- State offices

- Federal (United States) offices

GOVERNMENT OFFICES
  See listing in blue pages under U.S. Government,
  state or name of county or municipality;
  Libraries-Circulating and Rental; State Police; etc.

GRANDVIEW, CITY OF
  Police Department 555-9887
    Emergency: Dial 911
  Public Information 555-9886
    220 S. Hamilton
  Mayor 555-4586
    220 S. Hamilton
  Income Tax 555-2353
    220 S. Hamilton
  Parks & Recreation 555-0968
    100 Grandview

Recycling 555-0023
    220 S. Hamilton
Senior Center 555-1927
    480 Rocky Fork Boulevard
Water-Sewer-Trash 555-6529
    220 S. Hamilton

GRANITE
  Cosmic Granite & Marble 555-4321
    171 Granite Avenue

GRAPHIC DESIGNERS
  Abaez Design Inc. 555-0849
    6601 Broadway
  Anon Graphic Design 555-0556
  Art & Ideas 555-0617
    845 Boulevard East

A phone book tells you how to find government offices.

You can also check your phone book's Yellow Pages under Government for a listing of phone numbers. When you need some help, look through the government offices that are listed. Start with the level of government that you think you need, such as your city or county government. Call any information numbers you find that you think might help. Explain what you need. The person who answers this number may be able to help you.

Practice

Find the government section in your phone book. On a separate sheet of paper, list the main numbers for your town, county, state, and federal government offices.

22-3 ▶ Finding Help for Special Needs

Think back to Carly from the beginning of the chapter. She has a hearing problem. Her hearing problem makes talking on the phone difficult. The state where Carly lives offers a free relay service that would help her. This relay service passes messages along. The service makes it easier for people with speech or hearing problems to use the telephone.

Carly needs to get a machine called a **TTY**, which means "text telephone yoke." A TTY is also called a TDD, which stands for "telecommunications device for the deaf." A TTY is like a typewriter with a small screen for messages. Anyone can order one. You just have to call the number listed in the phone book under Services for Special Needs.

The relay service is easy to use. Carly types in a phone number on her TTY. An employee at the relay service then reads the phone number. The employee calls the number Carly typed. Carly then types a message to her friend. The relay service employee reads the message

Did You Know ?

A TTY is like "closed captioning" on a television. It allows a hearing-impaired person to read the words someone is speaking.

out loud to Carly's friend. Then the friend gives the employee a message for Carly. The employee types the message, and Carly reads it on her TTY. Carly can also use this service to order pizza or buy something over the phone. She can do anything with her phone that anyone else can do.

Other special equipment is available for people with special needs. One piece of equipment that is now used is designed for people who cannot use their hands. This machine allows them to blow puffs of air to dial phone numbers.

For more information about what is available, you can call local agencies. You can also look under Services for Special Needs in the phone book.

Maybe you or someone you know has a physical problem that makes it hard to get around. Many city buses are now equipped with wheelchair lifts. These lifts make it possible to get wheelchairs into and out of the buses.

Think About It

Why do you think communities offer services for people with special needs?

Many bus companies also have special vans. These vans pick up people at their homes. The vans take them anywhere they need to go. The charge for a trip is usually very low. Find out whether your community offers this kind of help. Call your city bus company to ask whether they offer the service.

Practice

Look through the list of community services in your phone book. Write down the phone numbers for emergencies, such as the number to call for an ambulance. Find the TTY numbers. Share what you find with a classmate.

Finding Things to Do With Your Free Time

Maybe you are just looking for something to do with your free time. Most communities have a **recreation** department or a parks and recreation department. Recreation means activities to do for fun. Your town's recreation department might organize sports teams. It might also offer special courses.

These activities are usually free or nearly free. Call your recreation department and ask about its activities, or look for an ad at your school or library.

Using Your Public Library

Libraries offer interesting things to do with your time. Many libraries lend CDs, audiotapes, and videotapes. Your library might sponsor programs for people your age. Ask for a list of the events your library is planning.

Doing research at the library can also be fun. Your library probably has computers that let you explore the Internet. You might also be able to use the library's **CD-ROM databases** to get information you need for school reports. A CD-ROM database is a computer laser disk filled with an enormous amount of information.

Locating People Who Share Your Interests

Your community newspaper can help you find people in your community who share your interests. Look for a section that lists special interest groups. This section might be called *Community Happenings, All Around Town,* or something similar. Each group listed will include a phone number. Look for groups that interest you.

Using Technology

Most libraries have card catalogs available on computer. These machines are set up throughout the library to allow people to find materials fast.

Practice

Research to find a group that shares one of your interests. Use the newspaper or ask people you know for information. Share what you learn with the class.

YOU DECIDE
How to Help a Neighbor

Read the situation below. Then follow the steps to help Lee decide what to do.

Lee's elderly neighbor, Mr. Rothman, lives alone since his wife died. He has always been friendly. Last month, Mr. Rothman had a stroke. Now he uses a wheelchair. Lee never sees him outside anymore.

Lee knows there must be services in the community that could help his neighbor get around. However, he does not know if he should suggest them. After all, Mr. Rothman is not part of his family.

On a separate sheet of paper, follow the steps below to help Lee make a wise decision.

STEP 1   Identify the decision Lee must make.

STEP 2   List Lee's choices.

STEP 3   Cross out any choices that are harmful or might be against Lee's beliefs.

STEP 4   Think about the possible results of the remaining choices.

STEP 5   Select the best choice.

STEP 6   Explain how Lee would carry out that choice.

STEP 7   Describe the possible results of Lee's choice.

Make a Difference
What advice would you give Lee about finding community services for Mr. Rothman?

Summary

You can use the telephone book to find out what services are available in your community. Most phone books list the phone numbers for community services in the front.

Phone books also list phone numbers for government agencies. Numbers are listed for city or town, county, state, and federal government offices. Sometimes the phone book has a chart that shows which agencies provide certain services.

A free relay service and a machine called a TTY or TDD help people with hearing and speech problems use the telephone. Bus companies have wheelchair lifts and special vans to help people with disabilities get around.

Community recreation departments offer low-cost activities, courses, and programs.

Public libraries lend not only books but also CDs and videotapes. Many also have computers that anyone can use to explore the Internet and gather information.

The newspaper often lists special interest groups. You can attend these meetings and get to know people who share your interests.

Vocabulary Review

agency

food stamps

recreation

CD-ROM database

TTY

Write the term from the list that matches each definition below. Use a separate sheet of paper.

1. a computer laser disk filled with an enormous amount of information

2. a department or office that works on certain issues

3. equipment that helps people with speech or hearing problems use the telephone

4. coupons issued by the government that can be used to buy food

5. activities to do for fun

Chapter Quiz

Write your answers in complete sentences.

1. What are three community services that might be listed in the front of your phone book?

2. What are three types of government agencies that a phone book lists?

3. What can you do if you do not know which government agency to call?

4. How does a person with a hearing loss send a message over a TTY?

5. Can a person who uses a wheelchair get to work on a city bus? If so, how?

6. It is summer and you want to play a team sport. How might you find one?

7. **CRITICAL THINKING** You want to learn about the Internet, but you do not have a computer. What are two things you could do?

Writing Activity

Does your community offer enough activities for young people? If yes, list them all. If not, explain why not. Think of ways you could convince the school board, city council, or another group to support more activities for young people. Write your ideas on a separate sheet of paper.

Group Activity

Work with a small group to list at least 20 low-cost things to do in your community. Start with things you and your friends do. Also, check the newspaper, your recreation department, and the public library. Read your list to the class.

Unit 7 **Review**

Read each sentence below. Then choose the letter that best completes each one.

1. Part of being a good citizen is
   A. voting in elections.
   B. not paying your taxes.
   C. getting out of jury duty.
   D. all of the above

2. Phone books list numbers for
   A. preparing taxes.
   B. government agencies.
   C. movie theaters.
   D. all of the above

3. Pedestrians should do all of the following, except
   A. cross streets at corners and crosswalks.
   B. hitchhike.
   C. follow the traffic signals.
   D. walk on the sidewalk.

4. Your yearly income tax form is due in
   A. January.
   B. April.
   C. December.
   D. June.

5. Some things that are NOT available in public libraries are
   A. books and magazines.
   B. audiotapes and videotapes.
   C. snacks.
   D. computers.

6. All bikes should have
   A. a noise-making device such as a bell or horn.
   B. good brakes.
   C. lights and reflectors for riding after dark.
   D. all of the above

7. Look in your community newspaper to find
   A. special interest groups.
   B. federal agency phone numbers.
   C. CD-ROM databases.
   D. TTY information.

8. If you have a car accident, you should NOT
   A. leave the scene.
   B. call the police.
   C. check to see if anyone is hurt.
   D. report the accident to your insurance company.

Critical Thinking
What are four things that a good citizen does?
WRITING Suppose a school bus stops in front of your car. Write a short paragraph listing what you should do.

Appendix

Glossary

Index

Glossary

action plan   a list of steps to help you reach a goal

addiction   a physical dependence on a drug

advice   suggestions about what should be done

aerobic exercise   an activity that makes your heart work harder

agency   a department or office that works on certain issues

ambulance   a special van driven by someone trained to help sick or hurt people and transport them to a hospital

ATM   an automatic teller machine; a machine that allows you to take money out or put money into your bank account using a special card

balance   the amount of money in a bank account

balanced diet   foods that provide your body with what it needs to stay healthy

bank statement   a report that the bank sends you to show how much money is in your accounts

bill   a written request for money for something you bought

blood pressure   the push of the blood as it moves through your body

body language   showing feelings using your body and your face

budget   a plan for spending money

calories   units that measure the amount of energy your body gets from food

candidate   a person running for an office in an election

car insurance   money you pay a company each month so that the company will pay for repairs after an accident

car pools   groups of people who share rides in each other's cars

career   the type of work a person does throughout his or her life to earn a living

career goal   the work you would like to be doing several years from now

career plan   a step-by-step way to reach a career goal

cash a check   to give a check to a bank and receive the amount of money written on it

cavity   a hole in a tooth caused by decay

CD-ROM database   a computer laser disk filled with an enormous amount of information

check   a written order directing a bank to pay a certain amount of money from the account of the person who signs it to the person named

check register   a small chart where you record the checks you write and the deposits you make

checking account   a bank account from which a depositor can withdraw money using a check or debit card

citizen   someone who lives in a certain city or nation

citizenship   active, helpful membership in a community

classified ads   advertisements listed in a special section of the newspaper

communicate   to share thoughts, feelings, and ideas with others

concern   an interest in other people

conflict   a strong disagreement caused by a difference in needs or points of view

consumer   someone who buys things

cosigner   a person who agrees to pay for someone else's credit card bill if that person cannot pay it

courage   the strength to stand up for what you know is right

cover letter   a letter to introduce you to an employer

co-workers   people who work for the same company

credit   money that you borrow from a bank, store, or credit card company to pay for things you buy

credit bureau   a business that puts together credit reports

credit card   a card that lets you buy something now but pay for it later

credit report   a report of whether you have paid your bills or loans on time

curfew   a time by which people must be home or off public property

deadline   the latest time something can be done

deduction   money taken out of a paycheck

defensive driving   driving carefully to avoid accidents

deposit   money put in a bank account

deposit slip   a form you fill out that shows how much money you are putting in the bank

diet   everything that you eat or drink regularly

down payment   the first payment on a large purchase such as a car

due date   the date by which a bill should be paid

emergency   a situation that needs to be taken care of quickly

emotions   feelings

employee handbook   a book that describes company rules and job benefits

endorse   to sign your name on the back of a check

exchange   a trade of one item for another

exemption   a tax deduction for each person in a family

expenses   payments

express   to show your thoughts, feelings, or ideas

false alarm   a warning about a danger that is not real

federal   national

fine   a fee a person must pay for breaking a law

fire extinguisher   a hand-held device used to spray special chemicals on a fire to put it out

fired   dismissed from a job

flexible   able to change

food stamps   coupons issued by the government that can be used to buy food

fumes   gases given off by chemicals

germs   tiny life forms that can cause disease

goal   something you want to do

gross pay   the total amount of money an employee earns

health   mental and physical wellness

health insurance   a plan that helps you pay for health care

honesty   the ability to be truthful and fair

hormones   chemicals in your body that cause and help control physical changes

housing   places where people live

impulse   a sudden act, done without thinking it through

income   the amount of money you earn

income tax   money that everyone who works pays to the government

independent   able to take care of yourself

informational interview   a discussion with someone who has a job that interests you, to learn more about that job

ingredients   the parts of a prepared food

interest   (1) something you care about or like to do; (2) money that a bank pays you for keeping your money in that bank; (3) a fee that you pay when you borrow money or a payment you receive when you keep your money in a bank account

interview   a meeting in which you answer another person's questions about yourself

issue   a question people make a decision on

job application   a form you fill out when applying for a job

job benefits   health insurance, vacation time, and other things you receive in addition to your salary

job review   a rating of how well you are doing on your job

jury   a group of people chosen to decide whether someone on trial is innocent or guilty

landlord   someone who owns a house or an apartment and rents it to others

late fee   an extra charge when a bill is not paid on time

layoff   a period of time when a company has no work for employees

littering   leaving garbage on public property or on someone else's property

loan   money borrowed from a bank and paid back in regular payments

long-term goal   a goal you expect to reach in several months or years

maiden name   a woman's last name before she is married

mature   adult

mechanic   a person who repairs car engines

medical license   a document that gives a person the right to provide health care

minimum   the lowest amount of money a depositor can keep in an account without being charged an additional fee

minimum payment   the smallest payment that will be accepted

mortgage   a loan used to buy a place to live

need   something you must have

negative   harmful, unsafe, or against the law

net pay   the amount of money an employee receives after deductions are taken out of the gross pay

nutrients   the parts of food that your body needs to grow and stay healthy

nutrition   the process of taking food into your body and using it for energy and growth

obstacle   something that stands in the way of reaching a goal

opinion   a belief

over-the-counter medicines medicines people can buy without a doctor's order; nonprescription drugs

patient   a person under the care of a doctor

paycheck   a check from your employer for the money earned from a job

paycheck stub   a form attached to a paycheck that lists important information

pedestrian   someone who is walking, running, or jogging

peer pressure   influence from people your age to do or not do something

personal qualities   ways you relate to other people and to the world around you

pharmacist   a person who prepares and gives out medicines that a doctor orders for you

point of view   a way of thinking about something

popular   admired or wanted as a friend

positive   helpful or healthful

prepared   ready

prepared food   food that is treated in some way so it will last longer

prescription   an order for medicine that a doctor provides

pressure   to strongly encourage

priority   a level of importance

promotion   a new job with more responsibility and more pay

public property   streets, highways, parks, playgrounds, and buildings that are open to all people

public transportation   a system of buses, trains, and subways that is available to everyone for a small fee

realistic   within your reach

receipt   a form that the bank gives you that shows how much money you put in or took out of your bank account

recreation   activities to do for fun

references   people who know you well and will tell employers that you are a good worker

refund   a return of money

register   to sign up to vote

rent   to pay an owner to live in a certain place

rental agreement   a written agreement between a renter and a landlord; a lease

resist   to refuse; to say "No"

respect   the willingness to consider other people's needs, feelings, and opinions

responsibility   the ability to be dependable, to make wise decisions, and to accept the results of your actions and decisions

résumé   a summary of your education and work experience

retirement   the years after a person stops working and earning income

risk   a chance that something harmful might happen

route   a certain path or direction

savings account   a bank account on which interest is paid and from which a person can withdraw money

schedule   a list of times to do things

security deposit   money that renters pay in case they damage their housing

service   to take care of a car's needs, such as changing the oil and adjusting the engine

service contract   a written promise by a store or company to fix a product if it breaks within a certain time

serving   the amount of a food usually eaten at one time

shift   a period of time for work

short-term goal   a goal you expect to reach in a few hours, days, or weeks

signature card   a card you sign when you open a bank account

skill   something you do well

smoke detector   a device that gives off a warning sound when it senses smoke

social security a government-run retirement savings program

Social Security number a number assigned to each person by the government; a form of identification

specialists doctors who treat only certain diseases or disorders

specific clearly described

standard deduction an amount of money set by the government for each income level; it can be subtracted from your income

stress uncomfortable feelings caused when you have too much to deal with

studio apartment a one-room apartment

summarize to explain briefly the main ideas of what you heard, saw, or read

summons a legal request

symptom a sign of illness or disorder

tax deduction a cost that can be subtracted from your income when you figure out your taxes

teller a bank employee who works behind the counter

temporary learner's permit permission to practice driving with a licensed driver in the car

traffic the movement of people and vehicles through an area

treat to work to cure or relieve a disease or disorder

TTY text telephone yoke; equipment that helps people with speech or hearing problems use the telephone

unit pricing how much a product costs per unit of weight or volume

vitamins types of nutrients your body needs to stay healthy

want something you would like but can do without

warranty a written promise that a product will work for a certain amount of time

withdrawal slip a form used to take money out of the bank

withheld held back; taken out

Index

A

Accidents. *See* car accidents
Action plan
    meaning of, 15, 19
    for reaching goals, 19–20
Addiction
    drug/alcohol/cigarettes, 94–96
    meaning of, 87, 95
Ads
    and buying behavior, 226–227
    for housing, 271, 275–276
Advice, meaning of, 41, 42
Aerobic exercise
    benefits of, 94
    meaning of, 87, 93
Agency, meaning of, 313, 315
Alcohol. *See* Drug/alcohol use
Ambulance, meaning of, 103, 108
Anger
    calming down, 60–61, 62
    making ourselves angry, 61–62
ATM (automatic teller machine), meaning of, 191, 194, 201
Attacking messages, nature of, 57–58

B

Balance, of checking account, 198–199
    meaning of, 191, 198
Balanced diet, meaning of, 87, 88
Bank statement, meaning of, 191, 202
Banking, 192–202
    bank statement, 191, 202
    cashing paycheck, 211–212
    check register, use of, 198–199
    check writing, 196–197
    checking accounts, 191, 193–194
    choosing bank, 199–200
    deposit slip, filling out, 195–196
    savings accounts, 191, 200–201
    transferring money, 214
Benefits. *See* employee benefits

B (second column)

Bicycle laws, 305
Bill, meaning of, 239, 240
Bill paying, 240–241
    due date on bill, 240–241
    late fees, 239, 240
    late payments, 241
Blood pressure, meaning of, 103, 106
Body language
    feelings expressed through, 46–47
    meaning of, 41, 46
Budget, 207, 212–218
    and future planning, 216–217
    and individual needs, 215–216
    meaning of, 207, 213
    set up for, 213
    and shopping, 225–226
    staying on, 214, 215

C

Calories, meaning of, 87, 91
Candidate, meaning of, 287, 291
Car accidents, 303–305
    actions to take, 304–305
    prevention of, 304
Car buying, 261–265
    car insurance, 255, 265
    dealer service, 262
    down payment, 263
    loans, 263–264
    mechanic check, 262
    paying for car, 263
    used car, 262
    warranty on car, 261
Car insurance, 255, 265
    cost of, 265
    factors affecting cost, 265
    meaning of, 255, 265
Car pools, meaning of, 255, 257
Car safety, 119
    drinking and driving, 266
    reckless driving, 265
    responsible drivers, qualities of, 265–266

Excuse, meaning of, 9
Exemptions, meaning of, 287, 293
Exercise, 94
    aerobic exercise, 94
Expenses, meaning of, 207, 212
Express, meaning of, 41, 43

F

Falls, in home, 117
False alarm
    as illegal act, 308
    meaning of, 301, 308
Family
    changes in, 73–77
    learning values from, 5–6
Federal, meaning of, 287, 292
Federal assistance
    finding services, 315–316
    food stamps, 313, 315
Feelings
    and body language, 46–47
    and hormones, 71
    and "I messages," 56–57, 58
Fees, for checking accounts, 193–194
Fine, meaning of, 301, 303
Fire safety, 115–117, 120–121
    and electrical wiring, 117
    fire extinguishers, 115, 121
    smoke detectors, 115–116
    steps to take during, 120–121
Fired, meaning of, 159, 162
Flexible, meaning of, 129, 133
Food Guide Pyramid, 88–89
Food labels, information on, 89–92
Food stamps, meaning of, 313, 314
Friends
    being part of group, 72
    changing friends, 72–73
    and decision making, 29–30
    finding friends, 30, 36–37
    importance of, 71–72
    peer pressure, 31–35
    qualities of a good friend, 30–31

Fumes, 117
Furnishing a home, 278–279

G

Germs, and disease, 87, 97
Goals
    action plan for reaching of, 19–20
    career goals, 175, 176–177, 180–181
    long-term goals, 15, 18
    meaning of, 15, 16
    obstacles to, 16
    and priorities, 15–16
    purpose of, 16–17, 22
    realistic goals, 17–18
    short-term goals, 15, 18
    specific goals, 17
Golden Rule, 48
Grocery store, shopping tips, 229–230
Gross pay, meaning of, 207, 210

H

Health
    addiction, 94–96
    and cleanliness, 97–98
    and doctors, 104–107
    emergencies and hospitals, 108–109
    and exercise, 94
    meaning of, 3, 5
    and medicine, 107–108
    and nutrition, 87–92
    safety tips, 97–98
Health insurance, 109–110
    function of, 109
    meaning of, 103, 109
    shopping for, 110
    types of policies, 110
Health Maintenance Organization, 110
Hearing problems
    and relay service, 316
    and TTY (text telephone yoke), 316
Home
    cleaning home, 279–280
    furnishing home, 278–279

Honesty
    meaning of, 3, 5
    and responsibility, 10
Hormones
    and emotions, 71
    meaning of, 69, 70
    functions of, 70
Housing
    buying housing, 273
    meaning of, 271
    renting housing, 272–278
    types of, 272
    See also Home

I

"I messages," to express feelings, 56–57, 58
Impulse, meaning of, 223, 229
Impulse buying, meaning of, 229–230
Income, meaning of, 129, 133
Income tax, meaning of, 287, 292
Independent, meaning of, 3, 11
Informational interview
    and job search, 136
    meaning of, 129, 136
Ingredients, meaning of, 87, 89
Insufficient funds, meaning of, 193
Insurance
    car insurance, 255, 265
    health insurance, 103, 109–110
Interest
    on checking accounts, 193
    on credit cards, 244–245
    on loans, 241
    meaning of, 191, 193, 239, 241
    on savings accounts, 200–201
Interests, meaning of, 129, 132
Internet
    and banking, 196, 200
    and car buying, 262
    and company information, 152
    and credit reports, 247
    and housing ads, 276
    and health information, 95
    and income tax forms, 295

and job listings, 138
and peer pressure, 31
and product information, 233
and public transportation, 256
and résumés, 145
Interview, meaning of, 143, 150
Issues, meaning of, 287, 291

J

Job application, meaning of, 143, 148
Job benefits, meaning of, 143, 159
Job interview, 150–153
    and needs of a person, 133–135
    and personal qualities, 131
    behavior during interview, 151–152
    post-interview steps, 153
    preparation for, 150–151
    references for, 147
    résumé, 144–146
    screening tests, 150
    and skills, 131
    "Want Ads," 138
Job review, meaning of, 175, 183
Job search
    choosing a job, 153
    information sources on, 136, 137–138
    and informational interview, 136
    and interests, 131–132
    job application, 148–150
Jobs
    versus career, 135, 175
    communication on job, 163–164
    computerized time clock, 168
    conflicts on, 164–166
    and co-workers, 160, 161
    deadlines, 169
    employee handbook, 159, 161
    first day at, 160–161
    job benefits, 154
    keeping job, 162–163, 170
    losing job, 170
    new skills, learning, 166–167
    promotion, 180–181

Temporary learner's permit, meaning of, 255, 260
Temporary work, 170
Time management
    planning guidelines, 20–22
    versus wasting time, 21–22
Traffic, meaning of, 301, 302
Traffic laws, purpose of, 303
Traffic tickets, points, 303
Transportation
    car pools, 257
    cars, 259–266
    public transportation, 255, 256–258
Treat, meaning of, 103, 106
TTY (text telephone yoke)
    function of, 316
    meaning of, 313, 316

U

Unit pricing, meaning of, 223, 230

V

Values, learning from family, 5–6
Vitamins
    functions of, 92
    meaning of, 87, 92
Volunteering, methods of, 296
Voting, 290–291
    and candidates, 291
    on issues, 291
    register to vote, 287, 290–291

W

Want, meaning of, 223, 224
"Want Ads," for jobs, 138
Warranty
    on car, 261
    meaning of, 223, 233
    on products, 223, 233–234
Water safety, 119–120
Weather, safety tips, 118
Withdrawal slip, meaning of, 191, 201
Withheld, meaning of, 287, 294
Withholding, taxes, 294

Photo Credits